A PERSONAL STORY OF SOMALILAND,
A COUNTRY THAT OFFICIALLY DOES NOT EXIST

INVISIBLE STATE

Jama Gulaid

Paperback ISBN: 9798990445307

Maps

Colonial Territories in Africa, 1914

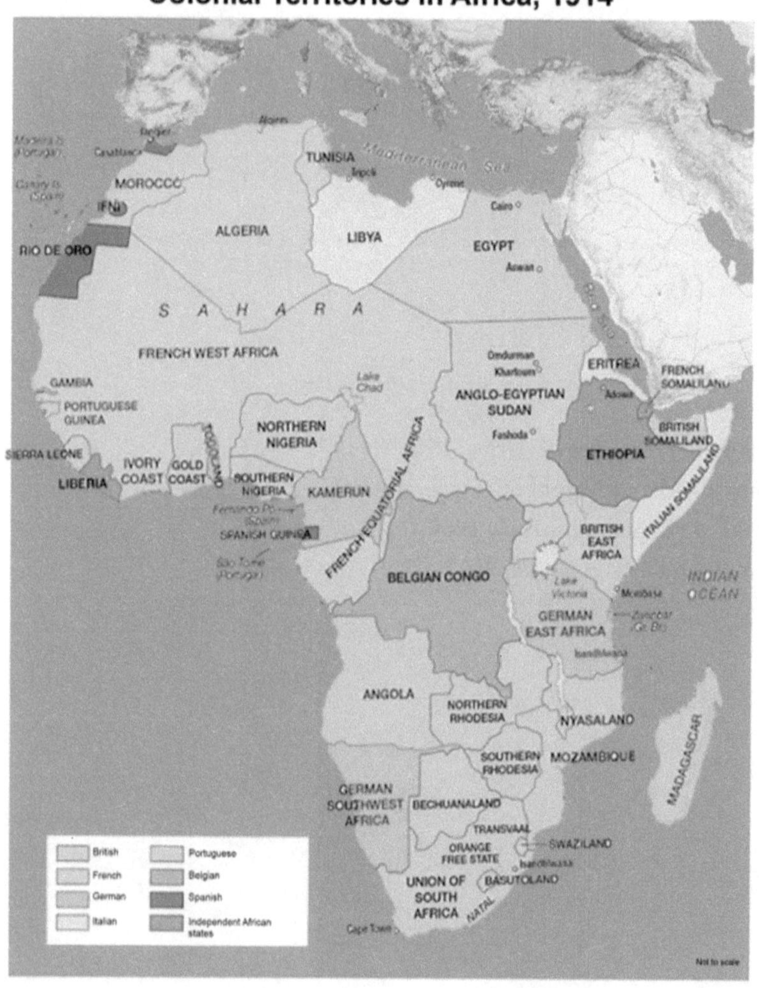

Somaliliand and Neighbouring Countries

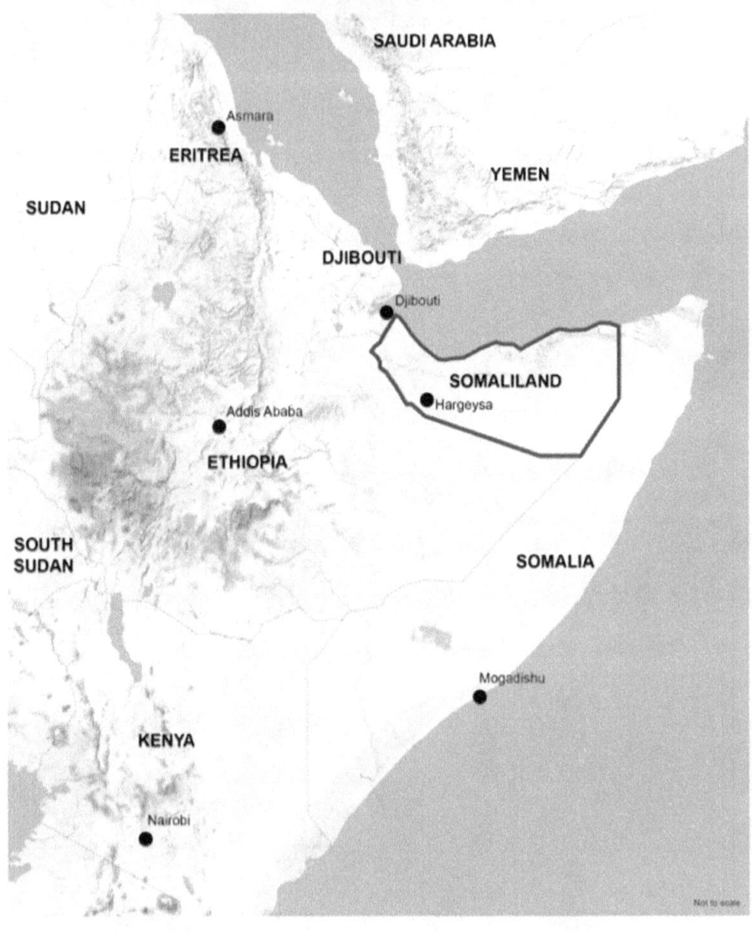

Isiolo to Hargeisa Journey, 1960

Major Towns in Somaliland and Places Visited in 2019

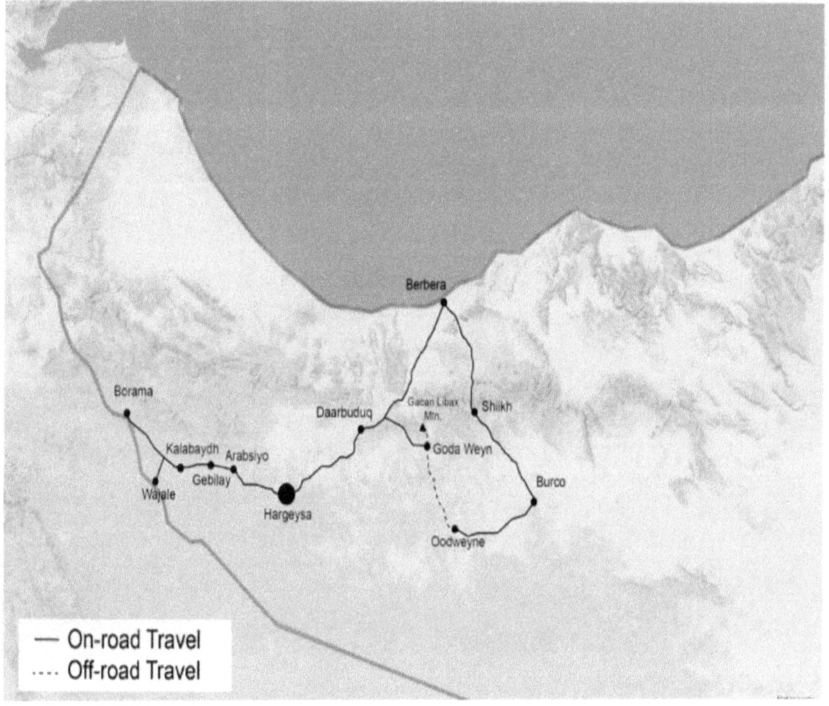

This book is for the women in my family who overcame
many challenges in the last fifty years and the youth who
deserve attention to thrive in a competitive world.

Contents

Acknowledgements

Telling this story was more complex than I had imagined. Richard Beynon and Jo-Anne Richards, my writing advisors, frequently returned my draft notes with the same comments, "Jama, show more emotion." I turned to my wife for consolation, and she echoed the same sentiment.

I protested that emotions do not come quickly to a nomad, even if the topic is emotive. My advisors just smiled and continued to offer valuable advice. Thank you, Richard Beynon, Jo-Anne Richards, and Laurie Gulaid for the helpful suggestions. Thank you, Cabdillaahi Xasan Fureh, for the encouragement to finish the work.

I am grateful to my wife, Laurie, and daughters, Mariam and Sofia, who cheered me on. Mariam travelled with me to Somaliland and is part of the story. Sofia was at school then, but she prepared the maps I used in the manuscript, except for the colonial Africa map, an adaptation from *Facing History and Ourselves* of Brookline, Massachusetts, USA.

I am also grateful to my faithful readers: Amina Axmed, Dr Axmed Magan, Cabdiraxmaan Madar, Ilhaan Jaamac, Laurie Gulaid, Mariam Gulaid, Sofia Gulaid, Xuseen Imaan, and Axmed Sharmaarke. Special thanks go to Saamiya Yuusuf, Dr Diriiye, and Max Gulaid for making the trip happen smoothly.

Dr Magan deserves special mention for his encouragement at all stages of the writing. More than anyone else, he understood the physical and emotional aspects of my journey to Somaliland. Cabdiraxmaan Madar provided much-needed editorial assistance with the Somali text. Thanks to Richard Dionne and Sara Bigley, who helped prepare the manuscript for publication. Thanks also to Saamiya Yuusuf, our hostess in Hargeysa.

Finally, I would like to thank the people featured in this story. With them, there are events and more to share. But any shortcoming from this work is solely mine.

What was driving me to write was the silence – so many
stories untold and unexamined.

Toni Morrison

Note on Somali Names

A note on three crucial names: Somaliland, Somalia, and the Somali Republic. Somaliland was a former British protectorate. Somalia was a former Italian colony. The Somali Republic is the name of the republic created from the union of British Somaliland and Somalia in 1960. Between 1960 and 1991, Somalia was the label often used in place of the formal name, the Somali Republic. Somaliland left the union with Somalia in 1991 and has revived its old name, Somaliland.

Where I have added English-language translation, these appear in italics beside the Somali text.

On names, I followed the convention of the script adopted for the Somali language in 1971 to benefit Somali readers. For readers from other countries, I have enclosed a rough transcription of the names that appear in the manuscript.

NEW SCRIPT	OLD SCRIPT
Aaden	Aden
Aftax	Aftah
Axmed	Axmed

Bacaw	Baaw
Bacadle	Baadle
Baaruud	Barud
Birjeex	Birjeh
Biixi	Bihi
Burco	Burao
Cabdala	Abdula
Cabdi	Abdi
Cabdirashiid	Abdirashid
Cabdile	Abdile
Cabdillaahi	Abdilahi
Cabdiraxmaan	Abdirahman
Cali	Ali
Cawyke	Awke
Caynabo	Ainabo
Ceel Xume	Eel Hume
Ceerigaabo	Erigabo
Cidin	Idin
Ciise	Essa
Cilmi	Elmi
Dhamac	Dama
Ducaale	Dualeh or Duale
Faarax	Farah
Faadumo	Fadumo
Foodcade	Fod Ade
Gaalkacayo	Galkayo
Gacma Dheere	Ga'ma Dhere
Gashaamo	Gashamo
Goroyo Xun	Goryohun
Hargeysa	Hargeisa
Ibraahin	Ibrahim
Il Carmo	Il Armo
Imaan	Iman
Ismaciil	Ismail

Jaamac	Jama
Jeclo	Je'lo
Kaahin	Kahin
Laas Caanood	Las Anod
Libaaxo	Libaho
Lixle	Lihle
Maxamed	Mohamed
Maxamuud	Mohamoud
Cumar	Omar
Oodweyne	Odweyne
Qorax	Qorah
Raxma	Rahma
Saamiya	Samiya
Saleebaan	Suleiman
Siciid	Said
Siyaad	Siyad
Taleex	Taleh
Timacade	Tima Ade
Weysacade	Weysa Ade
Xasan	Hassan
Xayd	Haid
Xuseen	Hussein
Xaaji	Haji
Xaajia	Hajia
Xaashi	Hashi

Introduction

One day in June 1960, a bus parked in front of my father's store in Isiolo, my birthplace in colonial Kenya. It was the only civilian vehicle in town and it attracted locals – young and old. Suddenly, I was the envy of all the boys.

The bus came from Tanganyika, another British colony. All the passengers were ethnic Somalis travelling to Mogadishu for the Independence Day celebrations of the Somali Republic. The big day was 1 July 1960.

My parents soon called me to the bus. "Do you want to ride it?" my father asked.

"Yes, Father. Yes."

"You know who will meet you on the other side?"

"No."

"Xasan, Xuseen, and Maxamuud."

"My brothers!" I said, jumping up and down on recognising the names of siblings I had never met. They left Isiolo for school in British Somaliland when I was too young to remember.

The mention of my three elder brothers was all the enticement I needed to ride the bus to an unknown destination. Thus, I became the bus's youngest traveller at age six.

In the Somali capital of Mogadishu, I met crowds larger than anything I had seen in Isiolo, and the city lights were more colourful than the night sky in my village. I also attended parades and celebrations.

Several months later, I found a new home and school in Oodweyne, a village southeast of Hargeysa. My schoolmates were all boys from the Somali-inhabited territories in the Horn of Africa. Ismail, a nephew, and I were the only two from British East Africa. Free education drew all of us to the Somali Republic.

Oodweyne had no cars, and there was no police station. The most frequent sounds were the call to prayer – and rooster cries. In the dry winter months, the faint songs of herdsmen watering their stock at the local wells added to the ambient noise.

I had three meals a day, new clothes every year, and one shilling of pocket money weekly from my guardian in Somalia.

Classes, eating, sleeping, and playing football with a tennis ball filled my days. At nightfall, I washed off the dust from the football field and had dates and camel milk for dinner before tackling my homework. I turned off the kerosene lamp by 9 pm and slept on a colourful Persian rug. The village clock ticked ever so quietly.

Periodically, the scanty rainfall came late or ended prematurely. Then we rationed water, and the imams prayed to Allah for relief. Altogether, the outside world did not intrude much into my daily routine.

During the school holidays, I travelled on a truck to Hargeysa. Since we had little to do, my friends and I made frequent forays on bikes into the Shacabaka, the old colonial hangout. The flight of foreigners was so fresh we could almost pick out their scent in the unguarded bungalows. Occasionally, we trudged across the narrow suspension bridge, the only structure straddling Waaheen, Hargeysa's seasonal river, called *tog* in Somali. The river came alive in the rainy season when flash floods swept everything. The thought of the shaky bridge and the sight of water churning under my feet still evoke motion sickness more than half a century later.

One summer, I spent the school holiday with relatives at a nomadic encampment on the Tuuyo Plain. My job was herding baby animals, the lowest rank in the hierarchy of jobs in the camp. I returned to school with stories of a milk diet, thunderstorms, and nights of sleeping under the stars except when it rained.

Most schoolboys in Oodweyne lived apart from their families like young male antelopes. The summer holidays gave them a reprieve from this solitary existence, but I envied my schoolmates when they visited their families. My nephew Ismail and I were 2,000 kilometres away from home. We waited six years for the first reunion with our parents.

I heard adult stories about independence and what it would do for people, but I only remembered one story – the promise of milk and honey.

I dismissed the first part of the story because milk was plentiful in our home. I paid attention to the honey part, however, because I liked sweet things such as candy, dates, and jaggery, the dark, unrefined sugar from the toddy palm sap of Asia.

I kept wondering about independence and honey. Who would deliver the syrup? Would it come in cans or milk jars? These and other questions popped into my head.

One day, I crossed paths with pale women in black robes with children in Hargeysa. "These are Algerians running from war," locals said while urging everyone to be generous with cash donations. One aspect of the Algerian story troubled me though. Independence got them war, not milk and honey. No one explained the anomaly to me, but I forgot about the whole affair after the Algerians moved on.

Then, in the mid-1960s, people talked about trouble in the Northern Frontier District (NFD) of Kenya, where my parents and sisters lived. I was a little older, so I noted this troubling episode and the outbreak of violence. Conflict and four years of emergency rule plunged the NFD into poverty. In the end, many inhabitants, including my parents, sought refuge outside the country.

The Somali Republic, my new home, had its share of turmoil. In 1969, a military junta toppled the civilian government and ruled the country for twenty-two years. When the military dictatorship fell in 1991, the firestorm swept everything in its path. The country was declared a failed state.

Now almost an adult, I followed the Somali experiment with self-rule. Independence started with a burst of euphoria. It also opened doors to schools for many people like me. I accepted this gift as a substitute for the honey I once dreamt about. But, unfortunately, the excitement of the early years was short-lived. Soldiers took control and trampled on the fragile democracy. Violence became their trademark. The country plunged into civil war.

In 1991, Somaliland, beaten and impoverished, rose from the ashes of the old Somali Republic. In 2019, I set out to see the country and reconnect with my relatives and the places I lived between the ages of six and eighteen. Here is the story of my trip.

PART I

Return

On 10 June 2019, I set out for Somaliland with my eldest daughter, Mariam. My last visit there was in 1984. Mariam was not born then, and Somalia, the country that Somaliland was part of, had not yet become a failed state.

I thought about the country I knew nearly a half-life ago. The thought prompted a flurry of questions: What kind of family reunion awaited us? Would it be difficult to reconnect with my friends from secondary school? What was the place like after the civil war?

The night before we departed from Nairobi, I tossed in bed. I did not recall ever feeling this way before a trip. An upbringing in a nomadic culture had blunted expressions of "softness." Travel and family separation were part of daily life. It was rare for family members to spend a whole year together.

My parents took this custom to an extreme. At six, they sent me across two colonial boundaries to attend school. We lived nearly 2,000 kilometres apart for six years without direct conversation.

More questions came to mind: Why the anxiety and sudden insomnia? Was it a reaction to talking with relatives who had survived the civil war? Was I getting soft or too sentimental?

Mariam had never set foot in a troubled or unstable country. She was born in New York City and grew up in Ghana, Vietnam, Swaziland, and the USA, where I set up camp as a United Nations employee.

I had another troubling thought whirling in my head. How would I explain the messy history of Somalia and Somaliland and the Ethiopian-Somali hostilities to my daughter? My mind was spinning. Share stories. Share stories… Then I drifted into sleep.

The next day, I picked up a suitcase, a camera bag, and a sufficient supply of my blood pressure medications. Let's see how the trip goes, I said to myself.

We flew with Ethiopian Airlines, the only foreign carrier offering a convenient service from East Africa. This carrier had two daily flights between Addis Ababa, Ethiopia, and Hargeysa, Somaliland.

Commercial links between the neighbouring countries were unimaginable during my childhood. Ethiopian Airlines started its historic flight to Somaliland in 2001. The decision demonstrated a seismic thaw in the relationship between the two societies with a history of clashes over territory. The people were quick to engage soon after the lifting of political barriers. In 2019, Mariam and I joined the merchants, students, and civilians taking advantage of the peace dividend.

We had a layover at Addis Ababa Bole, one of the busiest airports in Africa. At our terminal, we crossed paths with pilgrims from Mecca in ceremonial robes, Africans in colourful clothes, and Chinese and Indians in sneakers and tracksuits as if dressed by a single supplier. With so many people toting luggage with both arms, avoiding collisions with other travellers milling about in the departure hall was challenging.

"Let us find peace and coffee, Aabo," Mariam said. *Aabo* is the title a father and his offspring use to address each other.

"Good idea," I replied.

We retreated to an airport café. The scent of freshly brewed Ethiopian coffee greeted us. At that corner of the airport, I shared stories about the Somali-Ethiopian relationship.

"I once believed Ethiopians were the enemies of Somalis," I said. "Years later, I heard that Ethiopians thought the same of us. That is how I grew up in Somalia in the 1960s. Prejudice thrived on both sides of our common border."

Mariam stared at me. Her gaze softened when she realised I was talking about the past. I had barely started, so I continued narrating stories from the past, including one of an Ethiopian air raid of Hargeysa when I was a child.

"That day, two American-made F-86 Sabre aircraft swooped into town from the west and dropped bombs."

The incursion was a surprise and a novelty in Hargeysa. People who should have taken shelter wandered the streets. Their eyes scoured the southwestern horizon for a glimpse of the noisy planes. I tucked my flip-flops under my armpits and ran from our residence to join a crowd near Seketa Liire.

Fingers pointed west where thick smoke billowed. The planes struck the Locust Control Department camp, a branch of the United Nations responsible for controlling locusts. The agency maintained a depot a few kilometres southwest of the Hargeysa military command centre.

I recalled the sounds of thunder from the cloudless sky on the southern side of town near the airport. The unfamiliar noise came from the anti-aircraft batteries of the Somali Army.

Deep in my reminiscing, the public address system came alive. "Ethiopian flight 373 to Hargeysa is ready for boarding. All passengers proceed to the gate."

At 3:20 pm, we were airborne.

I gazed at the arid landscape stretching below us. Addis was 580 nautical kilometres from Hargeysa. Jigjiga, the closest town to Hargeysa, was 150 kilometres away! The territory below us was a no-go area all of my life. The sight triggered memories of another chapter of the Somali-Ethiopian relationship that Mariam had to know.

"Ethiopians and Somalis have a long history of clashes over territory and religion," I said, resuming my narrative. Then I gave her a brief account of the most recent territorial clash along our flight path. The war started in late 1977. Somali Armed Forces rolled east to claim the Ogaden region, which Imperial Britain had ceded to Emperor Menelik II of Ethiopia in 1897. The initial phase of the campaign was remarkably successful.

The Somali forces and their local allies captured nearly all the disputed territory except two towns, Harar and Dire Dawa. The pendulum swung the other way when Moscow ditched Somalia and provided massive aid to

Ethiopia. The Soviets airlifted in 18,000 Cuban special forces, 1,500 Soviet advisors, Yemeni fighters, T58 tanks, MiG-25 fighter planes, rocket launchers, and other sophisticated weapons to Ethiopia. The airlift was the largest that Africa had ever seen and the most intense that the Soviet Union had undertaken over a short time since World War II.

Somali President Maxamed Siyaad Barre had committed a strategic error. He cut ties with the Soviet Union. The decision enraged Moscow. The Soviet ambassador revealed the depth of Soviet anger at a press conference: "We will teach [the Somalis] a lesson they will not forget. We will bring them to their knees."

The Soviet power achieved its goal. Somalia lost the war. I told Mariam how I followed the war stories from Connecticut and Minnesota, USA. I also mentioned my one-year work with refugees of this conflict, starting a month after obtaining my Master of Public Health (MPH) degree from the School of Public Health at the University of Minnesota. I wanted to help, and the International Rescue Committee gave me such an opportunity.

In the Somali Republic, we had a medical team comprised of an American physician who was the leader, an American and a Belgian nurse, an American administrator, and me, the public health specialist. We also hired half a dozen young Somali youth to help us.

Our task was to look after the health of the refugees from Ogaden, the Somali-inhabited region of Ethiopia. The health team had no precise estimates of the population in the Malkahida refugee camp and the adjacent Suriye camp on the bank of the Juba River. The military authorities fudged the numbers to secure more aid for Somalia. But Malkahida's actual population could have been between 25,000-35,000. My friend, Dr Axmed Magan, was the head of the Refugee Health Unit of the National Refugee Council when I was there. Aware of the politics of numbers, we eschewed discussions of sensitive matters and focused on delivering essential health services using working figures of vulnerable populations – primarily children and pregnant women.

During my year with the refugees, I saw the impact of conflict on children and women. The camp was ghostly silent at the start of our work. Malaria, malnutrition, diarrhoea, and respiratory infections had sapped the inhabitants' energy, especially the children.

Many of the refugee families had lost young men in the Ogaden War. Others suffered after the armies stopped fighting. They were victims of the Ethiopian army's retribution against Ogaden's inhabitants, who were considered sympathetic to Somalia. Those who managed to escape and travel through the vast, waterless region ended up in the camp.

Our dedicated medical staff (Dr Rick Steketee and nurses Bic Wirtz and Rachel Mixer) ran clinics and therapeutic feeding centres six days a week. They also attended to people who showed up at our grass-roofed huts at odd hours with an emergency.

I trained rural health workers on sanitation practices, screened malnourished children, and mobilised communities to immunise their children from preventable diseases. We worked six days a week and ten hours daily, not counting the emergency calls the doctor and nurses attended. We had two days of rest and recovery (R&R) each month in Mogadishu, a day's drive away.

In six months, we streamlined our work in the camp. Sick patients had access to medical care, malnourished children had special centres that provided therapeutic feeding, and pregnant women had their own clinic. We also conducted campaigns to protect children from common childhood illnesses and organised teams to spray dwellings with residual insecticide to reduce malaria infections. The camp's traditional leaders, all men, helped us, especially with health promotion.

A year later, I left the camp for the University of Minnesota for further studies. I read widely about Ethiopia and Somalia. The library material painted a gloomy picture. Both countries were among the poorest in the world. Thousands of children never saw their fifth birthday, and many women died from preventable pregnancy-related conditions. Yet, Somali and Ethiopian leaders invested more resources in warfare than in lifesaving programmes.

My library routine elicited comments. Barbara and Clint Knudson, my wonderful host family in Minnesota, thought I was perpetually cramming for tests. They did not know my preoccupation with Ethiopian and Somali affairs and my despair over these two countries' investments in warfare when thousands of children starved and many women died in childbirth.

"We are landing shortly at the Hargeysa International Airport; please put your seat in the upright position and fasten your seat belt," the flight crew member announced.

I looked out the window. Brown buildings and narrow roads appeared on the horizon.

Hargeysa, a city with over one million inhabitants, is the capital of Somaliland. The airport sits on a plateau about ten kilometres from the centre. From there, the city stretches north to a valley to the east and west. The tog divides the town into two parts.

The airport is on the southern edge of town. It has low buildings and a long runway fit for the MiG jet fighters that the Soviet Union donated to Somalia during the Cold War.

A red, white, and green flag, the new symbol of Somaliland's independence, fluttered in the breeze. The aircraft door flung open. Mariam and I joined other passengers shuffling their way to the exit with a clutter of carry-on luggage.

At the aircraft door, I paused. Eyes shut, I took a deep breath of air. Suddenly, I felt light-headed. I grabbed the aeroplane door to steady myself.

I don't recall how long I stood until an anxious passenger nudged me. With an apology, I inched forward.

Inside the airport, I followed people who seemed to know their way. Halfway between the entrance door to the terminal and the immigration desk, a middle-aged man wearing a yellow flak jacket over a white sleeveless shirt approached me.

"Ma Jaamac Axmed Guleed baad tahay?" *Are you Jama Ahmed Gulaid?* he asked.

"Haa," *Yes*, I replied, hiding my surprise.

"Xuseen Dheere ayaad isu egtihiin." *You resemble Tall Xuseen.*

He referred to an elder brother, an army officer and a war veteran in the territory on our flight path from Addis Ababa.

My encounter with the man in the yellow jacket reminded me that I was home. Where else could a stranger sniff out my genetic heritage?

Mariam and I tagged along with the man to the immigration desk. "Soo dhowaada," a young man in a white sleeveless shirt said. *Welcome.* He collected two $50 US notes and promptly stamped our passports.

A sister, a nephew, and two cousins were waiting in the arrival area. They stood there with grins on their faces.

My daughter's eyes welled. I, too, had tears in my eyes but quickly wiped away the wetness on my face. No one uttered complete sentences. I heard only affirmations of relations – "Walalo, Abti, Edo!" *Brother. Uncle. Aunt!* We embraced.

My thirty-five-year separation from family and friends was finally over. In less than two hours, the plane that took off at Addis Ababa, Ethiopia, had breached the prejudice that had separated Somalis and Ethiopians for years.

The changes that had occurred over these years suddenly hit me. Three of the four architects of the crises in the Horn of Africa were gone – Mengistu of Ethiopia, Barre of the Somali Republic, and Brezhnev of the Soviet Union. The Somali and Ethiopian dictators had lost power, and the Soviet Union had collapsed.

We collected our luggage and headed for the Masalaha. This new neighbourhood had large, two-storey stone houses. Each new building had an ornate iron gate and a two-metre stone wall.

An hour after landing in Hargeysa, we sipped tea with relatives in one of these houses. The place where we stayed belonged to cousins who live in London. It was a four-bedroom stone house with beige furniture, matching window curtains, frills, and Persian rugs.

I looked around at the people sitting with us in the living room. The men were grey-haired or balding except for a nephew, and the cousin who served the tea was a toddler the last time I saw her.

"Waar ismaad bedelin timaha mooye," said Dr Diiriye. *You've not changed except for the grey hair.*

"Adiga qudhaatha igamaad lunteen, Diiriye," I replied. *And I could have picked you out of a crowd anytime.*

I had not seen Diiriye, a classmate who became a physician, since 1972.

On arrival, I told my folks about our encounter with the man in the yellow jacket. Diiriye smiled and said, "I asked him to look out for you. Am glad he spotted you easily."

"Inataadu wey kuu egtahay. Masha Allah!" said another. *Your daughter looks like you. God bless.*

"Walaal, Mariam, soo dhowaada," said my sister Amina as she took leave with her son Maxamed. "Iska nasta. Beri ayeynu isarki doonaa." *My brother, Mariam, welcome again. Get some rest. We'll see you tomorrow.*

My brother Maxamuud, Max for short, said he would arrange the trip to Go'da Weyn, our ancestral village, and Oodweyne and Sheekh, where I attended schools.

We talked for a while longer. On occasion, everyone spoke at once. Laughter filled the room, but occasionally there were awkward pauses in the conversation.

Mariam watched us intently, driven to read the expressions on our faces when we reverted to speaking Somali, which she had not mastered.

Finally, the long separation was over.

History

Mariam and I frequented the veranda of our residence in Hargeysa. The place gave us a clear view of a small garden, a mustard-coloured wall, a blue metal door leading to our neighbour's house, and the exuberant magenta-coloured bougainvillea draped over the wall.

The only sounds were the rustle of leaves, the occasional flapping of the tarpaulin covering the Toyota Land Cruiser parked in the yard, and the drone of aeroplanes at the nearby airport.

June is typically windy. Sipping tea, we wrapped ourselves in shawls until about eight in the morning. We chatted intermittently about different topics, including history.

"Remember my comment about Ethiopians being the enemy?" I asked one morning.

Mariam nodded.

"Now, I can tell you how my views changed."

Mariam nodded again.

"My first encounter with Ethiopians in the flesh was in Minneapolis, Minnesota. None of the students I met on campus fit the image of an enemy in my head. They greeted me in Amharic or politely tipped their heads.

'Hi,' I replied, unable to respond in vernacular. I also got used to the surprised looks when I couldn't answer greetings in local languages. One fellow liked my old two-door, the winter-tested Oldsmobile Cutlass. When I left Minneapolis to work with the Ogaden refugees, I sold it to him for $50 though I had bought it for $500 two years before."

I told Mariam about other memorable meetings with Ethiopians, professionals and traders in and outside Addis Ababa.

Had I not travelled abroad, I would have spent more time in the Horn when Somalia and Ethiopia were hurling insults and shells at each other across the long international border.

During this time, dictators had held sway in both countries for decades. These men exacted punishment on their people as they demonised their neighbours. The young were victims of geography, local politics, and a propaganda diet. As the Somalis say, the adult snake empowers the baby snake by spitting venom into its mouth.

Mariam had travelled a long way to see the country of her ancestors. She deserved to know the story of local dictators and their legacies. I had broached the subject although I spared her the gruesome details.

I concluded my narrative with stories about Ethiopian and Somali dictators and how they were more alike than not. Most of all, I focused on how much pain each had inflicted on his people.

Emperor Haile Selassie reigned over Ethiopia for forty-four years. His government covered up a humanitarian crisis in the early 1970s. Somehow, pictures of the Ethiopian famine leaked to the outside world. This episode triggered the collapse of Africa's ancient monarchy. Military officers seized government control. They dragged the emperor to jail where he died, presumably, from strangulation.

Colonel Mengistu Haile Mariam emerged as the leader of the Ethiopian military junta. Embracing Marxism and Leninism, Mengistu launched the Red Terror campaign. In a few years, the Marxist-inspired initiative had claimed the lives of tens of thousands of people, including intellectuals and students.

Mengistu waged two other wars – a protracted war against a guerrilla movement seeking the independence of Eritrea and a campaign against Somalis in the Ogaden region. Eritrea was a former Italian colony. Ethiopia federated with Eritrea in 1952 and annexed it in 1962. The Ogaden was a vast disputed territory in eastern Ethiopia.

The war effort in the North was futile because the Eritrean liberation movement was deeply entrenched in the country. Mengistu's benefactors, Moscow and Cuba, also refused to deploy troops there, but Ethiopia was victorious in the Ogaden region, thanks in large part to the massive Soviet presence and Cuban aid.

Mengistu's rule lasted nearly two decades. Bloodshed was the hallmark of his rule; however, the violence backfired. A rebel force under Meles Zenawi's leadership ousted him in 1991. Mengistu fled Addis Ababa for Zimbabwe where he still lives.

General Maxamed Siyaad Barre came to power in Somalia through a military coup d'état in 1969. Two years later, Barre accused several collaborators of treason and executed them. Then he turned on the clergy who opposed the adoption of a Marxist-Leninist ideology in a Muslim country.

In 1977, Barre invaded the Ogaden region of Ethiopia and failed, mainly due to poor political execution of the war effort. After the Ogaden War, he focused on domestic affairs, carrying out purges. He rounded up innocent people and sent them to jail or the gallows and pitted clans against other clans.

Northerners felt the brunt of Barre's violence. Barre unleashed the full might of the Somali forces to crush them. Somali warplanes that hit Hargeysa launched their sorties from the airport where we landed. The violence drove hundreds of thousands of displaced people across the border into Ethiopia.

Barre deployed two generals, a cousin and a son-in-law, to direct the repression of Northerners. He also hired South African and Rhodesian mercenaries as insurance against any Somali plot secretly opposed to the bombing raids against civilians or people contemplating defection.

Barre's behaviour forced many Northerners to revisit their definition of an enemy. Barre earned the contempt that people reserved for old foes. His aides gained infamy for the cruelty they inflicted in cities and on civilians. Meanwhile, the Ethiopians received praise for sheltering hundreds of thousands of Somalis from northern Somalia.

Barre's rule lasted twenty-two years, but his tenure ended in disgrace like that of his Ethiopian counterpart. He fled the country in 1991 and died abroad.

My niece, Saamiya, joined us on the veranda at the tail end of my story-telling. She listened for a while and then spoke.

"Adeer, kaalaya quraacda," she said. *Uncle, breakfast is ready.*

She served freshly cooked injera (local pancakes), olive oil, honey, fresh papaya, and cardamom-scented tea.

"Adeer, hada ma saliid baa la isticmaalaa," I said. *Niece, the olive oil is a new thing.*

"Haa, adeer. Saliid zetuunku waxeey bedeshey subagii." *Yes, Uncle. The olive oil replaces the ghee.*

In the past, people made their ghee or bought it from stores.

The recall of a problematic history left a bitter taste in my mouth. Saamiya's cinnamon and honey-flavoured tea was a poor antidote for my nausea. I was silent at the table. But Mariam was more gracious to our hostess.

"Saamiya, this is yummy," she said.

"But you didn't eat much," Saamiya responded.

Hargeysa

Over the next five days, we explored Hargeysa. The airport looked familiar but renovated. I recognised only the Town Council, a relic from colonial days.

This multi-storey building stood out because of its flat roof, stone walls, and arched doors. The stone façade and the mosaic pattern on the windows looked intact. Someone had painted the arched doors green, one of the Somaliland flag colours, to make it look current.

Elsewhere, multi-storey structures cast long shadows on the dwarfish old buildings, and hundreds of pedestrians, hawkers, and vehicles mingled in the narrow streets. A chalky film of dust hung in the air. Hargeysa had changed, but the heartbeat of the city, especially the clammer of people and traffic on the dusty streets, was unmistakably African. It took us forty minutes to drive from Masalaha to a house in Little Jigjiga, a distance of about ten kilometres.

Hargeysa had more than doubled its population and acquired a cosmopolitan flavour it lacked in the past. It now had a sizable community of Ethiopians who worked as barbers, farmhands, laboratory technicians, and university lecturers, among other occupations. I also ran into Egyptians, Yemenis, Kenyans, and Syrians around the city.

Admas University College and the Addis Ababa Medical University in Hargeysa have Ethiopian connections. Other joint Somali-foreign ventures include medical diagnostic centres, hospitals, and schools. The Somali-Ethiopian association has had one crucial non-commercial influence; it humanised people's perceptions of each other. Unlike my generation, today's youth might just be less prejudiced.

Hargeysa's weather reminded me of Southern California. The days were sunny, warm, and dry, and the nights cool and pleasant. To my surprise, however, it was safer than most other cities I had visited despite its recent civil war history.

At nightfall, the phenomenal growth of the town came into view. From my vantage point near Masalaha, shimmering light stretched far beyond the valley, the centre of old Hargeysa.

"What are your impressions?" asked a relative after our city tour.

"You have a big city, new memorials, and Ethiopians," I replied.

The Hargeysa Airport honoured Maxamed Ibraahin Cigaal, the second president of Somaliland. A neighbourhood in Dumbuluq and a clinic carried the name of Maxamed Moogeh, a famous singer in the 1970s. Several streets also bore the names of Somali National Movement (SNM) veterans.

The relative listened patiently and smiled. "Waa runtaa waanu disanay magaaalada laakin waxaa jira dad badan oo dhaawacan." *Yes, we've rebuilt the city, but there are many injured people in our midst.*

I knew "injured" was a polite reference to mental illness. "Xageey joogaan?" I asked. *Where are they?*

"Qaar suuqa ayey wareegaan. Qaar kalena cilaaj ama guryo ayaa lagu hayaa." *Some are wandering in the streets. Others are in Ilaajs or family homes.*

An Ilaaj is an informal centre where a family may commit an ill member in return for a fee. Ilaajis often use untrained staff to look after residents.

The reference to mental health did not surprise me. The problem had appeared in my reading before the trip. Al Jazeera, the Centre for Justice (USA), Action Against Armed Violence (United Kingdom), and a Somali journalist provided valuable accounts.

The drift of the conversation to mental health, a serious subject, unnerved me. I did not want to touch this subject so early in the trip although I knew mental health was a common public health problem in conflict zones. I gingerly retreated like a man negotiating landmines.

Max's Camp

After six days of getting to know the family and exploring Hargeysa, we were ready to move on.

"Go'da Weyn will be the first stop outside Hargeysa," said my brother.

Go'da Weyn is fourteen kilometres south of Gacan Libaax Mountain, one of the most picturesque landscapes in Somaliland. It lies east of Hargeysa and not too far as the crow flies from Sheekh and Oodwyene.

Go'da Weyn is our ancestral village. It is also the resting place of my father and Xaaji Yuusuf Iman, my guardian in Somalia (while I was six to eighteen years old). I had not been back since 1970 when my mother and I brought my father's body there for burial.

My father, who we addressed as Aabo, was born in Somaliland around 1894. His 1956 passport described his profession as "Serviceman." He was one of the men recruited by Britain in Somaliland. When World War I ended and the colonial government disbanded its troops, Aabo settled in Kenya like many other war veterans. *Alien Somalis* was the name the British used for persons with roots in Somaliland or Aden, Yemen.

In the post-war years, colonial administrators introduced restrictive laws on land use. They forced African populations into native reserves while demarcating most of Kenya's fertile lands to White settlers.

Before these laws took effect, Aabo set up a home in Meru, a town on the foothills of Mount Kenya. He had a shop and a thriving butchery that supplied meat to an army camp. Refusal to comply with the colonial poll tax probably cost him his business. He then moved north to Barsaloi where he traded livestock with the Samburu. The land ordinance laws caught up with him there, and the colonial authorities relocated him to the Isiolo, an area reserved for Alien Somalis.

Isiolo thus became Aabo's permanent residence. Over the years, he acquired one of the first provision stores in town and one of the largest herds of cattle and sheep. He lost everything during the 1964–1967 conflict in northern Kenya, known as the NFD. My father, mother, and youngest sister, Amina, a teenager, left Isiolo for Nairobi during the crisis. They used Aabo's back pain, presumably a spinal disk problem, to obtain a travel permit from a region under security lockdown to Nairobi. A small suitcase and Aabo's prayer rug were the only possessions they could bring.

In 1967, my parents and youngest sister sought refuge in Tanzania. A few months later, they fled to the Somali Republic and ultimately settled in the North, which Aabo had left as a youth. Aabo died in Hargeysa three years after his return to Somalia. We buried him in Go'da Weyn.

Our trip to Go'da Weyn began the next day. We had a convoy of two Toyota utility vehicles. My brother Max and his driver were in one; Mariam, Nuura (a niece), and I travelled in our rented vehicle with Maxamed, our driver. My brother led the way.

Max followed the Hargeysa-Berbera road and turned off right after Dhubato Village. Then we travelled off-road for an hour and a half before reaching Deri Maraa, the foothills of Gacan Libaax Mountain.

Gacan Libaax is part of the Golis mountain range that runs on the spine of Somaliland from Ceerigaabo in the east to Borama in the west. It is also the major watershed in the central area of Somaliland. Runoff from this range swells the togs that supply water to the Red Sea coast and south-central region, including Burco and Oodweyne.

Max's farm had a domed house with three spacious bedrooms, two baths, and floors covered with ornate tiles. A red tractor rested in a shed nearby. The veranda overlooked Gacan Libaax to the east and the flat, expansive landscape to the west. Several naked bulbs shed light in different corners of the farmhouse.

Shortly after arrival, Max sent someone to a nearby settlement. The fellow returned with a yellow plastic can.

"Camel milk, everyone?" he asked.

The call triggered childhood memories in Oodweyne and the livestock flocking to the waterhole. I could almost hear the camels' gurgles and picture the frothy milk relatives gave me when I did chores for them during their visit to the Oodweyne waterhole. Not as salty, sour camel milk is tart like ayran, the famous Turkish yoghurt drink.

"I want some," I said, declaring my interest.

There were no other takers. Mariam and Nuura were not keen on trying it. Nuura's refusal surprised me; she'd grown up in a town where camel milk was not part of the diet.

I drank the milk while the others snacked on nuts, dates, fruits, and tea from Hargeysa. I dipped into my sour milk for the next two nights because it did not need refrigeration.

Mariam and Nuura turned in early, but Max and I sat on the veranda, chatting late into the night. Separated for fourteen years, we had much ground to cover. He updated me on his family in Ottawa, Canada, and his post-retirement work in Somaliland. I told him about our relatives in Kenya and my retirement after twenty-seven years of service with the United Nations Children's Fund (UNICEF).

The civil war and its impact in this area were topics we did not broach. It was too painful. Naturally, we had many other things to discuss, personal and family-related. Once again, I convinced myself it was not time to dwell on civil war stories. *We will talk about this some other time,* I told myself.

I learnt more about the farm operation and the challenges Max faced. He grew oranges and corn and raised some livestock. Periodically, severe droughts destroyed his crops and killed his camels.

The farm helped me see my brother's aspirations in a new light. He was trying to turn arid land into a productive farm. I was confident that Max had the requisite skills because he had trained in agriculture in the United States and had adjusted to extreme weather conditions in his youth.

He spent ten years on the American prairies, including six winters in Laramie, Wyoming, and four in Champaign-Urbana, Illinois. After the USA, he worked for a few years in Somalia under military rule and then moved to Saudi Arabia. A retiree, he spends his time at his farm in Gacan Libaax.

Before Mariam and I set out for the trip, I asked Max if he needed anything from the United States. His needs were few. Books and T-shirts were all he needed. We bought what he wanted and threw in a baseball cap.

In sections of the farm, I saw grass half a metre tall swaying in the breeze. I took this as a sign of good rain, but the evidence was misleading. Max explained that the previous dry season was long and arduous. He kept track of setbacks but showed no sign of surrendering.

"But this year, things should be different," he said. "I have two new reservoirs. My water supply will last until the next rainy season."

Our drivers had their entertainment at a nearby shed. They munched khat, a mildly narcotic plant, and built grand plans as this recreational drug took effect.

Close to midnight, Max signalled the farmhands to turn off the generator. Moments later, darkness descended on the camp, the only place with artificial light within sight.

I lay under a mosquito net, waiting for sleep. An hour later, I was still awake. I knew why, and it was not the cricket buzzing outside my window. The problem was my mind. It replayed clips from my recent conversations in Hargeysa.

As the shrill of the crickets modulated, I told myself that I would find a strategy to engage people during the rest of the trip without kindling agony or anxiety. Before I fell asleep, I resolved to listen and observe well.

Go'da Weyn

We set off to Go'da Weyn, my ancestral village, the next day after morning tea. It took us forty-five minutes to get there.

Go'da Weyn is a small village on the Golis range. As the crow flies, it is thirty-five kilometres southwest of Sheekh's famous schools, seventy-five kilometres south of Berbera Port, seventy-five kilometres west of the cultural and livestock commercial hub of Burao, and ninety-five kilometres east of Somaliland's capital. Besides proximity to centres of commerce and learning in Somaliland, the area offers rich grazing for livestock, the primary livelihood for local inhabitants.

My ancestors spent the rainy seasons around Go'da Weyn. They migrated south with their livestock to the Haud region in the dry season. The arrival of a colonial emissary irrevocably disrupted the migration patterns of the Somali nomads, including my ancestors. The emissary, Sir Rennell Rodd, went to Addis Ababa to negotiate a territorial deal with Emperor Menelik II of Ethiopia at the height of the European Scramble for Africa. He signed the Anglo-Ethiopian Treaty with the emperor in 1897. Neither of the treaty's signatories consulted the inhabitants whose land they divided. The treaty split the traditional grazing lands of Somali nomads. A large part of this territory went to Ethiopia. Britain turned the rest of the Somali lands into a British protectorate. This arrangement lasted for nearly seventy years.

Every government on this land has left a mark on the area. The British, who established rule in Somaliland in 1884, carved the gravel road linking the eastern and western parts of the protectorate through Go'da Weyn. They also built a mountain retreat for colonial administrators in Gacan Libaax; however, they ignored local requests for a borehole, school, and clinic.

Haji Yusuf Iman, the local MP, financed the construction of the primary school in the early 1960s. The military government diverted the vital east-west road away from Go'da Weyn in the 1980s. It also maintained troops around Go'da Weyn to intercept SNM forces or intimidate SNM's local sympathisers. After the junta's fall, the Somaliland government established a secondary school and a first clinic. President Axmed Siilaanyo also designated Go'da Weyn as a district.

Maxamuud Cabdillahi Guuleed, the local Go'da Weyn parliamentarian, received us on arrival. Others were on hand, but I recognised only two men – the elementary school's headmaster and a cousin, Cabdi. The last time I saw Cabdi was in 1972. He was an apprentice mechanic on a banana plantation in Balcad, a farming centre near Mogadishu. Insecurity drove him to Somaliland.

The old cemetery on the east side of the village was closed. The scarcity of people I knew made me acutely aware of the effects of time. All the relatives who helped my mother and me with my father's funeral in 1970 had died, adding to the cemetery population.

In the nearly fifty years since my last visit, Go'da Weyn had grown. The village's population increased during Barre's rule. Most people who settled here were internally displaced. To waves of poor, Go'da Weyn offered sanctuary and belonging.

The growth threatened the local cemetery where our elders rested. Concerned about the town encroachment, Max teamed up with the daughters and sons of Xaaji Yuusuf Iman. They hired village builders to put up a one-and-a-half-metre tall brick fence around the cemetery. Max was seeing the finished work for the first time. I saw him grinning as he inspected the work.

A villager promptly arrived with a key to the metallic cemetery door. Guuleed led the way. Max, Mariam, Nuura, and I followed him single file. About thirty metres inside the walled cemetery, our guide stopped and pointed to a spot with sisal plants.

"Odayaashii halkan ayey ku aasanyihiin," he said. *The elders are resting here.*

He referred to my Uncle Xaaji Imaan, my father, and Xaaji Yuusuf, my elder cousin and caretaker in the Somali Republic.

Mariam knew the story of how Aabo got here. Hooyo and I buried him next to his brother in Go'da Weyn, as he had requested. Thirty years later, Xaaji Yuusuf passed away. The challenge of bringing the body to Go'da Weyn fell on Max in Jeddah, Saudi Arabia. Remotely, he arranged the transport of Xaaji Yuusuf's body from London to Go'da Weyn. Xaaji Yuusuf's sons and daughter helped him. The task would have been difficult without the outstanding support of Daallo Airlines, a local carrier.

Faadumo Iman, a cousin, was the last of my relatives to rest in the Go'da Weyn cemetery. She died in Oodweyne and, like my father, had requested a burial next to her brother, Xaaji Yuusuf. The wish materialised. Standing there, I realised my duty to tell the younger generation about the bond among older family members.

We stood silently in a half-circle near the graves for about ten minutes: two sons, two granddaughters, and other relatives. We read verses of the Quran, as is the practice at a cemetery.

Because of the looting during the NFD crisis and the loss of Xaaji Yuusuf's priceless photo archives in Hargeysa, my family has only one photo of my father. We made copies and circulated them widely, but there were more enduring memories of him and the other elders at this cemetery. They grasped the value of education and were generous.

At that moment, I remembered a story my sister Caasha told me.

"Aabo and Uncle Xaaji Imaan cooked up the plan to send boys to Somaliland when they saw the restriction which the colonial government in Kenya had imposed on Somali communities."

That conversation between the two brothers set the stage for transferring seven boys to Somaliland between 1948 and 1960. Three of the fellows were my siblings. Three others were my nephews.

In 1948, Xaaji Yuusuf, the eldest son of my uncle, went to Isiolo, then a British colony, to fetch my eldest sibling, Xasan. Eight years later, Aabo escorted the second batch of learners. In 1960, my half-brother, Aw Tahir, escorted the last batch of children. I was a member of this last group.

"Xaaji Imaan did not live long enough to see the fruition of his ideas," I told Mariam. "He died in 1954. Implementation of the plan fell on Xaaji Yuusuf, who assumed guardianship of all of us from Kenya. I could not have asked for a better mentor and protector."

I wished the elders resting in the cemetery were alive. I would have given them a report card.

Max and I obtained PhDs from American universities. Mariam and Nuura, the two granddaughters with us on this trip, had earned master's degrees in public health, each by the age of twenty-five. My youngest sister, whom we left in Hargeysa, went to college, and so did all of her children.

An elder brother, Xuseen Dheere, contributed to another sphere. Trained in commando operations, he fought for the Somali Republic during the Ogaden War from 1977–78. Years later, he joined the SNM to help dislodge Barre's repressive regime from Somaliland.

Xasan, another sibling senior to Xuseen, attended the Mons Officer Cadet School in Aldershot, United Kingdom. He returned to Kenya and received further training at the Kiganjo Police Training College near Nyeri. In 1963, independence found him in Lodwar in the Turkana region. As the commanding officer in this rural outpost, he supervised the raising of the new Kenyan flag.

Two of my nephews studied administration. They worked with oil companies in Saudi Arabia for years, and then one returned to Somaliland to join the SNM.

Our visit to the cemetery was short. I picked up a silent message from the deceased relatives: to stay close to those I love.

Heroes

A store sign in Go'da Weyn read LIXLE PHARMACY in blue and red ink. The structure carrying the sign peaked through a gap in the cluster of buildings on the main street, unabashed by a sagging veranda. The sign was one man's tribute to a local hero, Maxamed Xaashi Diiriye, nicknamed Lixle. Before adopting a script for the Somali language in 1971, the name was written phonetically as Lihle. The village also named its only secondary school after this man.

Lixle (pronounced Lihle with a sharp h) was born in Go'da Weyn. He attended schools in Burco and Sheekh. After secondary school, he went to the Soviet Union to train in the maintenance and repair of mechanised military vehicles such as tanks. On his return to Somalia, Lixle taught at the National Military Academy in Kismayo, earning respect from his peers for diligence, vision, and strategic thinking. Lixle was a veteran of the Ogaden War and one of the founders of the military arm of the SNM.

The movement had one central objective – the liberation of Somaliland from Barre's brutal regime. The group established offices in the United Kingdom, the Middle East, and Ethiopia and has an operational centre for its military activities in eastern Ethiopia. This centre is near Somaliland.

Gaining followers was a dangerous thing during the dictatorship of General Barre. Lixle, who reached the rank of colonel, was a marked man. He was under surveillance by security services. Like a parolee, he needed a permit to leave Mogadishu. This treatment alienated Lixle.

In 1981, Lixle resigned from the army and returned to Somaliland to work undercover. He collaborated with like-minded officers and other residents of the North to end Barre's repression in Somaliland.

In late 1982, Lixle devised the raid on the Mandheera Central Prison to release political prisoners. Mandheera is about seventy kilometres south of Berbera. Barre's government used it as a hold-point for political prisoners. The Mandheera Raid was SNM's first and one of the most daring operations. The plan called for an incursion deep into Somaliland, releasing the inmates and returning to base undetected. Had the camp commander known of the threat, he could have crushed the SNM attack force using state resources at Cadaadley, a commando base barely thirty kilometres southeast of the prison.

The Mandheera Raid is a household story in Somaliland. I had to catch up on the details of this operation, so I read *Astaan Halgan*, Jaamac Cali Xasan's informative book on Lixle. I also watched video footage curated by local TV stations, such as Horn Cable TV and SAAB TV, which provided valuable information on the operation.

One of the TV informants was Xayd Garbadh, and another was Cabdiraxmaan Kaydsane Bulbul, the youngest member of the SNM unit that carried out the Mandheera jailbreak. The third was Axmed Xuseen Cilmi (Qorax) of Deri Maraa, a village on the foothills of Gacan Libaax. Of these three, I only met Qorax when my brother Max and I were touring villages near Go'da Weyn. Qorax helped Lixle with surveillance of the target and food delivery to the operations team when the men were hiding in mountain caves.

Garbadh was a captain in the Somali Air Force and a pilot for the military commander of the Northwest Region of Somalia. He left his job a few weeks before the commencement of the Mandheera operation. He was a secret collaborator with Lixle.

I talked to him on the phone twice while preparing this manuscript. In short, this is how the operation unfolded: Gashaamo, a village about fifty kilometres into Ethiopia, was a base from which the SNM launched attacks on troops loyal to Barre. Mandheera, the target, was seventy kilometres deep inside Somalia.

The fighters represented a small unit without reliable transport and modern communication equipment. But what they lacked in material things, they made up for in other ways – an unwavering commitment to the cause of liberation, familiarity with the terrain, and trust in local inhabitants.

Barre's forces knew of Gashaamo. The base was tantalisingly close to the Somali border and yet too far. It was too far in political terms because an attack on Gashaamo meant an incursion into Ethiopian territory. The act would elicit a similar response from the regular Ethiopian forces.

In mid-December 1983, the SNM Command Centre in Gashaamo hand-picked thirty-nine to forty-five fighters for the mission. Among them were three officers – Xayd Garbadh, Cabdiraxmaan Maxamed Case, and Maxamed Cabdi Aaden (Summuni). Garbadh, a captain and former pilot of the north-west military command, was the liaison between Lixle, the mastermind of the raid, and SNM leaders in the zone of operations and its leadership in Ethiopia.

From Burco, Garbadh secretly crossed into Ethiopia on a truck. He picked the attack force and sneaked across the border, again undetected. All of these movements took place at night.

On leaving Gashaamo, Bulbul said the fighters had no idea where they were going. Some assumed they were candidates for further military training, possibly in Libya, and that Addis Ababa was the first stop. It is plausible that someone concocted the Libya story to conceal the purpose of the top-secret operation. Only the officers (Garbadh, Case, and Aaden) had the correct information.

The truck limped from the start of this mission. The driver repaired it and continued the journey to the rendezvous with Lixle. At Goroyo Xun, the troops' vehicle made a sharp turn and headed north to Somaliland. Past midnight, the truck reached Go'da Weyn, where it stopped to fill a leaky radiator. There, the team crossed paths with a large contingent of Somali forces moving from southern Somalia to bases in the North.

"Who are you?" one of the soldiers from this contingent asked the members of Lixle's team who had gone to a spot in Go'da Weyn to draw water.

"Waxaanu nahay ciyaartooy ka yimid koonfur," Aaden replied. *We're athletes from the South.*

Bulbul said the concealment of their true identity worked. He attributed this escape to the frequent troop movement occurring at the time.

The assault team proceeded to Daldawan, a tog originating on the foothills of Gacan Libaax, thirty kilometres west of Go'da Weyn. Lixle had chosen this place as the rendezvous point. The truck had only one headlight. Lixle had decided on this feature to distinguish it from other traffic. When the one-eyed truck reached the river, Commander Lixle and several escorts materialised from the darkness. Another witness recalled that flashlights alerted Lixle of the truck's approach to the staging area.

As the troops dismounted, Lixle informed the truck driver that he had done his work. It was time to return to Gashaamo. The truck was loaded with limestone to disguise its mission, and then it departed.

Lixle and his aides led the men north up the river's course. I walked the path one day for several hours with a local guide. Rainwater had scarred the mountain's slopes, creating steep banks along the route. An hour later, my guide pointed his finger at a cave on the south-facing slope of Gacan Libaax and said, "Lixle and his troops hid there."

The route made a perfect hideout for anyone reaching Gacan Libaax Mountain. Even in daylight, no one could easily spot the vehicle my driver had parked in the middle of Daldawan.

Lixle had turned one of the many caves into a hideout. With the help of a few collaborators, he had stocked up on provisions, combat gear, and other vital supplies. It took the men a few hours to hike from the drop-off point to the hideout.

For the next nine days, the men rested and prepared for the operation. Lixle had the help of local collaborators in meeting the force's nutritional needs.

One day, Lixle addressed the group. "Mandheera Jail is our target," he said.

After the group meeting, he had one-on-one meetings with each member.

Lixle had conducted detailed groundwork. He had spent several months in the operation zone, disguised as a herdsman once, a farmer, or a pious traveller on other occasions.

He gathered intelligence on the Mandheera Prison set-up and security personnel, command structure, troop movements, and other vital information about the village and its terrain. He also had a prison map and information on the correctional officers' routines.

On 1 January 1983, the assault team ventured out of the cave. They were in fatigues identical to those of the Somali National Army. Carrying AK-47s, hand grenades, and bazookas, the men trekked through the hills to the Berbera-Hargeysa road where they lay waiting for road traffic.

The men needed a vehicle for the trip to Mandheera and later to escape with the freed prisoners. They wanted a small car like a Jeep for the job, and hijacking was their strategy for getting it. They took positions at Sheekh Abdaal, a village on the Berbera-Hargeysa Road. Abdaal is twenty kilometres north of Mandheera, the final destination of the assault team.

Berbera-Hargeysa road had light traffic that night, and none of the vehicles they stopped was suitable for the operation. The men continued their vigil. Meanwhile, the clock ticked towards dawn when the team would lose the element of surprise or risk discovery. At about 3 am, Lixle reached a decision. The men scrambled and took a trailer truck. They tied up the driver and his aides and dumped them in the back of the vehicle. A member of the assault team took the driver's seat and, with Lixle sitting by his side, headed for Mandheera.

The truck carrying the men halted at a roadblock near the camp, about five hundred metres from the military base in Mandheera. Two guardsmen with assault rifles approached the truck cabin, one from each side, asking questions about the cargo.

Lixle, who wore an officer's uniform, told the guardsmen that the vehicle was carrying prisoners. One of the guardsmen grew suspicious. He insisted that they step down. Moments later, he fired a shot. Lixle and his team retaliated. They fatally dispatched the two guardsmen.

One of Lixle's men took a bullet in his thigh in that first scuffle. Another bullet hit one of the front tyres of the truck, so the men abandoned the vehicle and pushed on.

Past the roadblock, the assault team split into two groups. The larger contingent, under Case and Aaden, approached the military camp. Lixle, Garbadh, and the other members of the assault team headed for the prison.

Although the gunfire at the guard post had alerted the rest of the sleepy town, the assault team moved at lightning speed. They struck their first target before the camp residents had rallied. More gunfire ensued. The noise startled the sleepy men. Some succumbed to the gunfire; others hid or ran away. In fifteen minutes, one part of the operation was complete. The military camp was in chaos, and the armoury was on fire. The team leader called Lixle by radio to share the news.

At the prison compound, the advance was slower. Thick metal barriers mounted at the prison entrance impeded the assault team. Then came gunfire from the guardsmen perched at the prison watchtowers.

Alerted by the gunshots, the guardsmen trained their weapons on the prison gate, firing at every shadow lurking in the dimly lit prison entrance. While coping with these challenges, other shooters attacked Lixle's team from behind. These were members of the Red Turbans, a well-trained crack team assigned to protect the area. Lixle had information on the 250 Red Turbans and the armed correctional officers who lived near the prison compound. They were slow in helping the soldiers on the military base, so they attacked Lixle's unit from behind.

Lixle and Garbadh called for reinforcements. The response was immediate. A group of the men that had hit the camp on arrival rushed to the prison area and neutralised the Red Turban attack. The reprieve allowed Lixle's team to tackle the remaining obstacles.

Now reinforced, Lixle and Garbadh pushed their team forward. They lobbed hand grenades at the prison watchtowers, blowing up the structures and the men hiding there. They then used bazookas to break the metal barrier blocking the entrance. Inside the compound, they used wrenches and sledgehammers to break the heavy locks on the prison cells.

In thirty minutes, the raid was over. The assault team secured their prize – eleven political prisoners. Two of the men had medical conditions and could not walk. They opted to stay behind for fear of hindering the escape of the others. The other nine men walked free.

The casualty rate was low. Two members of the assault team sustained injuries. One had a bullet wound to the chest; the other had been shot in the leg at the first roadblock. A paramedic from the assault team took charge of the wounded men. This group then disappeared with help from local sympathisers.

The assault team, with nine political prisoners in tow, headed for the tog to the east of the prison gate. Right on the eastern bank was a hill with access to the rugged Golis range. The terrain offered an escape route to freedom.

The prisoners and their escort reached the hills under cover of darkness. Hundreds of other inmates in jail also gained freedom that night. These men, too, had to find a way out of Mandheera or risk capture.

At daybreak, the government poured reinforcements from Berbera and the commando base in Cadaadley. Reconnaissance planes hovered over Mandheera and hills nearby shortly after sunrise.

Lixle sent two men to take the freed prisoners to another hideout. He stayed behind with the rest of the assault team. By midday, Lixle and his team clashed with two units of the Somali National Army.

One force approached Mandheera from the north. Another contingent advanced from Cadaadley. Lixle's team hid in the hills east of Mandheera. This position gave them a commanding view of the areas from which Barre's forces launched their counterattack. The mountain offered another strategic advantage during the skirmish: it provided access to the Golis Mountain range, where the SNM could hide among local sympathisers.

An exchange of gunfire occurred intermittently. Late in the afternoon, fog descended on the hills, covering Lixle's team. Under this blanket, the prisoners and the assault team hastened their escape.

On my visit to Mandheera, a guardsman stopped me from taking photographs, but I had snapped a few pictures before the man caught up with me. These were critical shots. They showed the prison's proximity to the Mandheera River, the escape route that Lixle had chosen.

The river was some 400 metres east of the prison gate. Then came a hill on the opposite bank of the river. Beyond that landmark lay the Golis range, Gacan Libaax, and freedom.

The Mandheera Prison raid was a milestone in the people's struggle in Somaliland. It showed government vulnerability. It also boosted the morale of the opposition group and inspired similar operations.

On the opposite side of the road from the LIXLE PHARMACY, I saw the faded sign of the Xaaji Yuusuf Imaan Primary School. The school, made of stone and with a flat roof, honours Xaaji Yuusuf, a man with a passion for education. Locals credit him with opening schools in Go'da Weyn and Oodweyne, two rural areas in central Somaliland. He sponsored more than two dozen young people, including my family members. His descendants support the school even though most live outside the country.

The school is the alma mater of Xayd Garbadh, the brave and enigmatic aid to Lixle. Garbadh joined the Somali Army as a cadet. He trained as a pilot in the Soviet Union. He also went to Italy for additional instruction and became a pilot for General Maxamed Xaashi Gaani, Siyaad Barre's cousin.

While flying General Gaani, Garbadh worked clandestinely with Lixle and others seeking an end to Barre's authoritarian rule. He walked away from his job when he learnt that Gaani had approved the arrest of Lixle for sedition.

Xayd and I knew each other well from Sheekh Intermediate School. We parted ways in 1968 and had not seen or talked to each other since then. In October 2020, I watched a remembrance video on Horn Cable TV.

"Today, my guest is a former pilot in the Somali Air Force," said Maxamuud Cabdi Ducaale, the veteran journalist and host of the popular Horn Cable show. "He's also known as Ina Xayd Garbadh, and he went to school in Go'da Weyn Oodweyne and Sheekh."

I knew only one Garbadh. I wondered if he was the same person. I called my nephew, Xuseen Iman, who lives near me now in Nairobi.

"Xuseen, guess what I learnt today?" I said, not expecting an answer to my rhetorical question. "The story of Xayd Garbadh and his role in the Mandheera Prison raid."

"Yes?" he said without interrupting.

"I went to school with someone with that name fifty-one years ago."

"Adeer, waa ninkii aad taqaaney," he said. *Uncle, your schoolmate is the one who became a pilot.*

The Garbadh I saw on the screen looked different from the young fellow in shorts. He wore a grey suit, white shirt, and a tie on the set. His hair was grey.

"Do you think he is still alive? The video is from 2015," I said.

"I knew he was in the United Kingdom, perhaps in Birmingham. I'll call Foosiya. She will know."

Foosiya is Xuseen's sister, one of the last Somali physicians to have left Digfeer Hospital in Mogadishu at the height of the civil war. She lives in London.

Xuseen sent me a WhatsApp message with Garbadh's number several days later. I called the same day I got it.

"Hello?" said a man on the other side of the line.

"Asalama Caleeykum. Ma Garbadh baa?" *Greetings. Is this Garbadh?*

"Caleeykum wa salaam. Waa isagiiye, waa kuma?" *Greetings. Yes, who is calling?*

"Waa Jaamac Axmed Guuleed. Bal waraan?" *This is Jama Ahmed Gulaid. How are you?*

"Waaryaa Jaamac, manooshahay? Waa lakala lumey." *Greetings, Jama. Are you well? We lost touch.*

"Ma ixususantahay?" *Do you remember me?*

"Aad iyo aad. Ardey wanaagsan oo salaada tukada ayaad aheeyd, waan xasuunahay." *Yes, indeed. You were a good student, I remember. You also went to the mosque regularly.*

"And you turned out to be a braver man than I."

"Waa waajib aanu iska ridney," he said. *We just fulfilled our duty.*

Garbadh and I were on the phone for an hour. We bounced information back and forth. I explained how I found out about him. He told me about his family and his experience as a teacher in the United Kingdom until retirement.

The man had multiple identities: a pilot in the Somali Army, an SNM intelligence officer, and a teacher in the UK. What a résumé!

I wanted to ask him questions about the Mandheera Raid but refrained from doing so in our first conversation in fifty-plus years. Ducaale of the HCTV had already covered the topic well.

"I'll come for a visit after the COVID epidemic," I promised and hung up.

"Insha Allah," he replied.

In March 2021, I called Garbadh again. He took the call and answered my questions about the Mandheera Prison raid.

"Garbadh, I have a few questions about Mandheera," I said. "I want to know about your trip back. What was your charge, and how long did it take you to return to base?"

"After the raid, we split into two groups. Summuni and Bulbul accompanied the nine men we released from prison. A nurse took responsibility for the injured men. Lixle, Case, and I stayed with the other members of the assault team.

"A short while later, Lixle and I separated. With an escort, he headed for Burco to connect with SNM operatives and report on the mission's outcome.

"I took the rest of the troops with me. As the last group to leave the area, we engaged government forces intermittently. We did this to delay the enemy and buy time for our colleagues to get away."

Lixle followed tracks through the Golis Mountain range to reach Burco, about 100 kilometres away. The freed prisoners, Garbadh, and the escort had a longer distance to cover – about 200 kilometres, mostly over open countryside with sparse vegetation.

"How long did it take you to cross this distance?"

"Twelve days. We walked at night and rested during the daylight hours. We could have travelled faster, but that would have been risky. We wanted the men to conserve energy for a possible clash with Barre's troops."

"How did the mission conclude?"

"Lixle reached Burco safely. So did the other two parties – the freed prisoners and the raid team. The injured men recovered and ultimately joined us in Gashaamo."

"One more thing, Garbadh. Aaden, whom you refer to as Summuni, did he study law at the El Azhar University in Egypt?"

"Yes!"

"Incredible! I met him in 1972 in Cairo. At the Somali Students' Association Club."

"Really?"

"He was one of the student leaders, a jovial fellow."

"That is the man. He completed his studies, returned to Somalia, and became a qaadi [a judge in the Islamic court system]. He joined SNM later to seek justice by other means. And he became an incredible fighter."

"What a small world! Is he alive?"

"No. I think he died in Sheekh shortly after our victory."

"So sorry. Did Summuni leave a family behind?"

"A wife and a son, I think."

"Tell me, Garbadh, did you get vaccinations against COVID-19?" I asked, changing the subject to the newest threat to our lives.

"Yes, my wife and I had the vaccinations, Alhamdulillah."

"That's great," I said, happy to note that this brave veteran had protection from the COVID threat. "We are still waiting for vaccinations here. Hopefully, we'll get our jabs soon, and then I can keep the promise of a visit this summer."

"Insha Allah."

"Thank you so much, Garbadh. Keep well."

•••

Before leaving Go'da Weyn, I requested a brief stop at the health centre. Having worked in public health since the rollout of childhood vaccines in Africa, I couldn't pass up the opportunity to see the first health centre in my ancestral village.

The centre hid behind a perimeter wall. I walked into a courtyard with an L-shaped building and a salmon-coloured roof. The one bougainvillea shrub in the compound glowed in purple. It made me wonder if bougainvillea would be the only ornamental flower I would see during the trip.

It was midday. The clients had gone, giving the clinic staff a moment to breathe.

"Haye, iska warama?" I asked. *How are you?*

"Waa nabad." *We're at peace.*

"Shaqada caruurta ayaan ubartey, markaa waxaan is idhi shaqaalaha kili-iniga soomar oo weydii xaaladu sidey tahay inta aanad tegin." *I've worked with children, and I couldn't leave without saying hello and finding out how things are.*

A young man in a white coat answered me. "Dawadii talaalku wey taal. Dawooyinka kale ee caadiga ahaana wey yalaan. Taageerana waanu kahelaa dadka degaanka," he said. *We have vaccines for children and pregnant women and the essential drugs. We also have support from the local communities.*

I asked if I could take photos of the charts he had posted on the walls. He nodded.

The clinic story was easy to read by looking at the charts. On average, twenty-one patients showed up daily. There were special services for children and pregnant women. The antenatal clinic (ANC) had an above-average performance rate; however, either a third of the pregnant women did not return for a third check-up during pregnancy, or they did not start antenatal care early enough to have a third visit before delivery.

Over ninety per cent of the children in the area had received the recommended vaccination. If correct, these findings would put the clinic among the top performers in the country. It is also plausible that population estimates were incorrect.

The clinic also provided other essential services to children: deworming, vitamin A and zinc supplementation, and malnutrition screening.

The most common medical complaints were acute respiratory infections (ARI), urinary tract infections (UTIs), pneumonia, anaemia, and diarrhoea. Eight per cent of the children screened had moderate malnutrition, which we expect to see where acute diarrhoea is among the top five diseases.

The clinic served 22,960 people in thirteen rural settlements around Go'da Weyn.

"Well done on your achievements," I said. "Such services didn't exist when I was a child."

The clinic attendant was smiling when we said goodbye. For a moment, he had the company of someone interested in his work, a break from his routine of seeing only patients.

The rebellion against Barre had a strong following in Go'da Weyn and the surrounding areas. The locals paid a price for their stand with the Somaliland National Movement. Barre's government exacted a heavy punishment on the civilians, especially after the Mandheera Raid. The village of Deri Maraa was the worst affected. The clinic is a mark of progress in a zone with little social and economic investment for a long time.

Gacan Libaax

After paying our respects at the family graves and a brief stop at the health clinic in Go'da Weyn, we left for Gacan Libaax, a mountain known in Somali as Lion's Paw. My brother arranged a traditional feast there. He secured the help of women from the village in the preparations. The fourteen kilometres took us nearly an hour of driving. We were tossed much of the way.

I did not see signs anywhere – only a bush fence marking the zone where livestock rearing was not permissible. The British had built a retreat there. Next to the colonial building, which had collapsed, was a low structure with concrete and iron sheets and two traditional houses with thatched roofs called *munduls*.

On arrival, someone led Mariam, Nuura, and Guuleed's daughter to the munduls. Another person directed the men to mats in the shade of a large juniper tree.

We had about an hour before lunch. I used the time to visit the toilet, a spacious room with a gaping window overlooking dense vegetation. A wasp drifted in and circled above my head. Unable to ignore the drone, I hastened my toilet visit but got a sting on my eyelid on my retreat. I yanked the glasses off my face and ran outside.

In the open, I walked to a stand with soap and water. I scrubbed my hands and splashed water on my face to soothe the surging pain. The last thing I needed was an insect bite reaction that would spoil my trip.

Mariam noticed my agitation. She stopped what she was doing and was by my side instantly.

"I have antihistamine and Tylenol tablets, Dad." Then she rushed to the mundul and returned with her handbag.

I swallowed the pills, sprinkled more water on my face, and thanked her for the first aid. Then I re-joined the men.

The pain receded like frostbite. Thanks to Mariam, who always packs essential medicines for trips, I had fully recovered by lunchtime.

Two men sat around large enamel plates heaped with food. This offering was a typical Somali feast: slow-cooked lamb and goat meat, rice pilaf prepared in the Indian style, pasta with minced meat sauce (a recipe adapted from Italian colonialists in southern Somalia), and stew. Broth with herbs and sweet tea came last.

At one point, I went to the mundul to check on the women dining separately.

"All is well, Aabo," Mariam said. "How is the bite?"

"Fine," I replied.

I said thank you to the women who had prepared the feast for us.

"We have to show you the caves," said Guuleed. "You can't come here and not see them."

After lunch, we hiked to the Gacan Libaax caves.

"Malaa habluhu meeshan ma geli karaan?" said Guuleed. *Perhaps this place may be inaccessible to the girls.*

We fell into a single file, ignoring the comment.

Deep inside one of the caves, a burst of light poured in through a slit at the top. That beam vanished in the belly of the cave, just like a flaming stick thrust into a fire eater's mouth. Mariam remembered to use a cell phone to light her path. The rest of us copied her example, and suddenly, five or six lights flickered in the darkness. We moved deeper into the cave until our babble disturbed the resident bats. Then came the squeals. Soon after, we made a hasty retreat although we did not encounter any offensive smell during our exploration.

Max and Guuleed selected the homestead of Bayle, my sixth-generation grandfather, as our next stop.

After just fifteen minutes on the move, our convoy of cars halted. We followed our guides to a cliff's edge and enjoyed a panoramic view of the terrain stretching below us to the Red Sea about thirty-five to forty kilometres to the north.

Max's knowledge of the area impressed me. He pointed out what seemed like an ancient encampment. The site had rocks arranged in a circle, delineating the perimeter of an old settlement.

"This is the homestead of Bayle, our ancestor," he said. "At that spot is Bayle Kamaag." Bayle's Retreat. He was pointing at the cliff facing north. We pulled back from the cliff, entered our ancestors' sacred compound, and took pictures.

The story has it that Bayle refused to set up his nuptial house at the bottom of the cliff. He selected a spot that commanded an unparalleled view of the environment: the grazing land to the south and the lowlands to the north.

At about 3:30 pm, we left Gacan Libaax for Go'da Weyn. Our stop there was brief. We sat under the California pepper trees, which Xaaji Yuusuf introduced to this village. Although old, they continued to sprout waxy green leaves and strings of colourful pepper-like seeds. After tea with a few locals, we left for Max's farmhouse.

A kilometre out of town, a woman waved us to stop. She wore a long dress with a floral pattern, a dark scarf for her hair as married women did, a light shawl on the shoulder, and a pair of leather sandals on her feet. Women dressed like her before all-black attire from Saudi Arabia and Iran arrived.

"She wants a ride to her camp," said the driver.

I said OK, and she hopped into the middle seat with Mariam and Nuura.

"Walaal xagaad kusocotaa?" I asked. *Sister, where are you going?*

The driver, however, had already guessed her mission.

"Reerki ayaa yaala meel aan foogeyn," she said. *The homestead is near here.*

"Anagu marti baanu nahay," I said. *We are visitors.*

"Iney martiyi imaneyso waanu maqalay." *I heard of visitors coming.*

"Roobku waa sidey sanad kan?" *How is the rainfall this season?*

"Aad buu ufiicanyahay." *It is good.*

We quickly covered the distance to her camp. The woman pointed to a homestead about a kilometre away.

"Walaal ayaal waad mahadsantihiin." *Brothers and sisters, thank you.*

Small bundles of sugar, rice, and tea were her purchases from the previous village.

We saw her camp bathed in the late afternoon sun. There were two traditional Somali huts and an animal pen. The huts were circular structures with arched sticks providing the frame and handwoven grass mats serving as walls and roofs. White sheep with black heads foraged on the hill nearby, and three camels stood amid the flock of sheep, like adults among children.

The woman and the homestead were reminders of my ancestors' lifestyle, which had not changed dramatically.

Country Road

In the old days, the dirt road passing through Go'da Weyn was the primary link between Hargeysa and Burco. I travelled on this route many times. The earliest was in 1960. The bus I boarded in Isiolo, Kenya, brought me to Hargeysa via Go'da Weyn.

The importance of this route declined in 1982 with the construction of a paved road linking Burao, Berbera, and Hargeysa. The new highway bypassed Go'da Weyn, leaving the village isolated. Today, most travellers from Hargeysa to Oodweyne take the long but smooth road via Berbera, Sheekh, and Burco. Another gravel road linking Oodweyne, Go'da Weyn, Mandheera, and Berbera has disappeared, adding to the village's isolation.

"It'll take us about four to five hours to reach Oodweyne," said Max. We gritted our teeth at the thought of bouncing in a four-wheel-drive vehicle for half a day but concealed our lack of enthusiasm.

"Forget the old road," said Guuleed, who went with us. "There is a better way. We'll follow the tog and reach Oodweyne in an hour."

We gladly fell in with the new proposal. However, the thought occurred to me that it was the rainy season, and these dry watercourses could quickly turn into raging torrents.

Much of the track was smooth. The river was fifty to one hundred metres wide from bank to bank and filled with coarse river sand. Past floods had compacted the sand and churned clay to the surfaces in patches. Under the blazing sun, the mud curled into flakes that cracked under our feet the few times we stopped to stretch our legs.

Our driver, Maxamed, was a slender fellow in his forties with curly hair. He was my point of reference during the trip and always had an intelligent answer. He chewed khat during our travels. Sections of our route were new to him and, in such places, he played every part the tourist like the rest of us.

At Gacan Libaax, I saw him earnestly taking panoramic videos, tripping once on the rocks because he was engrossed. Travelling in the tog meant bumps if the driver did not follow the grain of the sand. I held on to the handlebar above the door and looked to Maxamed for reassurance. I saw him videotaping the track with a smartphone as he drove.

"Maxamed, waa sidee?" I asked. *Maxamed, what is going on?*

"Waxba male," he said. *No worries.*

He continued taping.

"Waar halis baad nagelineeysaa. Naga jooji sawirkan." *You're putting us in danger. Stop taking photos while driving.*

Maxamed put away the phone and focused on driving. The vehicle continued its cruise at about fifty kilometres per hour. We all gazed out in silence.

"Waa gob," I said moments later, pointing at the crest of large evergreen trees lining the riverbank.

"Waa run," the driver said, confirming my observation.

Gob (*Ziziphus mauritiana*) is an indigenous evergreen tree that grows five to ten metres tall. Once a year, it produces yellowish-orange berries the size of coffee beans. People and goats cherish them.

The sighting of familiar vegetation rekindled memories of a childhood in Oodweyne. Hargeysa had an abundance of gob trees in the 1960s. I had not seen them before this leg of the trip.

Nearby, the picture looked different. Flash floods had scoured the river's bend and exposed the roots like eroded gums. One giant tree lay on its side, and another hung on by a thread. I imagined them tipping over next year when the tog swells with water again.

After about an hour of travel, the lead vehicle left the riverbed heading east. The rest of us followed. After a fifteen-minute drive through the scrubland, we entered a village. This was Oodweyne. Guuleed's prediction proved correct. We made the journey in an hour and a half, including stops for photos. Maxamed reverted to the calm and careful disposition I witnessed at the start of the journey. The rest of the trip was free of tension.

Oodweyne is a village with deep wells that attract nomads and their herds during the dry months of the year. It is an oasis with acacias instead of palm trees.

Here we drove into a hotel compound. "Let's get breakfast," said Guuleed. I wasn't hungry, but I was craving caffeine.

A young man met us there. He had only one helper, so he doubled up as a waiter, cook, and cashier. He offered minced meat sautéed with onion and tomatoes, homemade baguettes, and tea. He offered sautéed sweet peas from a can with onion and bread to those looking for a meat substitute.

We forgot to order water, so I went to the kitchen only to find a quarter of a camel's carcass dangling from a hook. I wanted to talk with the cook but could not see anyone. A rattle of plates drew me to a one-room building in the compound. That was the kitchen.

"Can you bring us drinking water, please?" I asked.

"Haa," he answered in the affirmative without looking up. He was preparing shah (tea) for us. I had never seen anyone doing it his way, so I paused to watch.

The cook started with a generous scoop of fine-grain black tea, compacted the powder with a tamper like a barista would use, and then turned on the espresso machine. A minute later, drips of tea concentrate trickled into a small vessel. The espresso machine hissed as steam bubbled through the milk holder. He poured the concentrate into two cups, adding a generous serving of steamed foam. Voilà! My first expresso tea was ready, robust, and flavourful.

Tea brewing had changed. The old tea masters in Oodweyne had no machines. They boiled the water, milk, tea, sugar, and cardamom in a large pot and served the mixture in porcelain cups with saucers.

While others enjoyed breakfast, my thoughts focused on the imminent return to my old school. My emotions tossed from excitement about a place

I had not seen since 1963 to anxiety about the combined effects of time and the Somali civil war on the school.

Oodweyne

A man toting an AK-47 met us at my old primary school gate. The school hid behind a high wall, and we had driven past it at first. The guard opened the gate only after our host explained the purpose of our visit. I asked him why he held such a lethal weapon.

"Third graders are writing their national examinations," he said. "My gun is a warning to anyone tempted to cause trouble."

A teacher in the school joined us for the tour and confirmed the guard's statement. How life had changed. In my childhood, I never saw anyone with a gun in Oodweyne. The village had a two-three man police station.

I scanned the compound and picked out the L-shaped stone structure where I spent three childhood years. Something about it did not look right. Then the teacher addressed the question running through my head and said, "Yes, the government added three new classrooms."

The beautiful stonework from sixty years ago and the extension looked great.

I entered one of the rooms and saw wooden desks identical to those I used. The furniture named the donors: UNHCR, the United Nations Commission for Refugees, and CHLE (Candlelight for Health and Education).

Everything looked familiar: the wooden benches, the windows, and the small blackboard. The only real change that had happened was in me. I had to edge sideways to squeeze into one of the desks and slide my long legs under the desktop.

Vivid memories of childhood flashed through my mind. I recalled sitting in that room and squinting at the teacher because I had trachoma, a common eye infection in rural places like Oodweyne. I could hardly make out the writing on the board when I was young.

I then understood the truth in the old Somali proverb: "Wadiiqada yari wadada weyn aye kugu ridaa." *The narrow path leads you to the main one.*

My baby steps in the three-room building started a journey that led me to better schools. I moved to Sheekh Schools first, then Trinity College in Hartford, Connecticut, and finally to Minnesota.

Brushes with illness also pushed me into a career in health. I studied public health for decades and combated childhood diseases, injuries, and violence. I was a beneficiary of a system that unashamedly favoured boys, but I had returned to Oodweyne with a daughter who had graduated from Columbia University, one of the top US universities in New York City.

Standing near the classroom door, my daughter smiled at me. Her voice snapped me out of my thoughts.

"Aabo, hold on for a photo," Mariam said as she pointed the iPhone at me.

A few minutes later, the photo was circulating on the internet.

We noticed a few broken windows and some overgrown aloe bushes. Not too bad, I thought, for a school in a country that had survived decades of neglect and civil war.

I recalled a story about my school's early history. Setting up a school for the children of nomads was difficult. There were no boarding facilities, so parents rented rooms in the adobe homes of Oodweyne for their children. I remember this arrangement very well. Some children lived in groups of three or four in rented rooms.

There is another story, however, that depicts the local interest in formal education. I had heard that every family with a child at the elementary school in the early years had brought a camel to Oodweyne to supply milk to their son. This strategy was sustainable and culturally appropriate. The children were familiar with a predominantly milk diet. Camel milk does not require refrigeration. The supply lasted throughout the school year because a camel can sustain milk production for twelve to eighteen months.

Two things reassured parents about the general welfare of their children. First, every child had a guardian in the village, some sharing the arrangement with several other children. Second, the boys, often ten to fourteen years old on enrolment in the first grade, were already used to hardship. The nomadic life had prepared them well for solitary, independent living.

When I arrived at Oodweyne in 1960, the old arrangements had changed. Oodweyne had become a larger village with more retail shops and teahouses. Nearly one-half of the children in my class rented adobe homes. They obtained their injera breakfasts, lunches, camel milk, and dates from local retail shops and teashops. Fresh camel milk was plentiful when this waterhole attracted large herds in the dry months.

One of my classmates at this school was Dayib Gurey. I remember him as a left-handed, skinny, likeable fellow. And he was fearless. We played football matches barefoot with a tennis ball as a substitute for the typical ball. Fifty-five years since we parted ways, I found references to him in Hargeysa.

Dayib joined the Somali Army, trained in the Soviet Union, and became a major. He joined the SNM and held important posts. In May 1988, Dayib was a member of the war council of the SNM force that launched the daring offensive against Barre's troops in Hargeysa. Dayib fought side by side with the current president of Somaliland, Muuse Biixi, and my elder brother, Xuseen Dheere, in the vicious battle for control of the city. After the rebirth of Somaliland, Dayib became a member of the cabinet. He died in 2006, and a large school in Dumbuluq, Hargeysa, was named after him.

One of the two male teachers giving us the tour of my old school spoke to me as we prepared to leave.

"We made a new addition," he said, pointing at a row of classrooms made of concrete bricks. "The students are taking their examinations there."

We retraced our steps to the parking area, hoping not to overexcite the gun-toting guard or disturb the students.

On the same day, I visited the intermediate school, which opened in 1963, three years after Somaliland had gained independence. At that time, the country had a civilian government that tried to show the fruits of freedom to an adoring public.

The school could have been my alma mater, but luck, a government decision, and a generous relative changed that. The intake of new students in 1963 was twice the size of a regular class. This decision overstretched the capacity of the school. It forced the government to find a temporary home for the children from Oodweyne. My classmates and I went to Ber to wait for a signal to return to our old village. Before this happened, Xaaji Yuusuf had arranged my transfer to Sheekh.

The Oodweyne Intermediate School occupies a large area about two kilometres out of town. The community protected the buildings and put a fence around the school's perimeter to prevent village encroachment. Sun, dust, wind, and seasonal rain have tested the structures for over fifty years, yet the buildings seem to have survived in decent shape. The flag of Somaliland fluttered on a pole planted at the centre of the campus.

More recently, the community secured help from locals to install solar panels to generate electricity. The most significant development of the last half-century, however, was the change to the admission policy allowing girls to attend school. "Girls and Boys Can Succeed," read a bold inscription on the administration building.

There were few signs of neglect. Tables in the chef's room and near the service window had heavy grease, dried blood, and grime stains. The stove and fireplace looked like the underbelly of an old diesel engine.

A man I presumed to be a watchman addressed us.

"Waryaadha iskuulka wax kusoo kordhiya hadaad wax ka barateen," he said. *Donate if you attended this school.*

He then pointed to the rooftop solar panels.

"Waa hadal wanaagsan, laakin anigu iskuulkan kamaan bixin," I said. *That's a good idea, but I didn't attend this school.*

I was asserting my allegiance to the elementary school nearby.

As we drove away, I knew the school needed assistance, and I had to contribute.

•••

We returned to the hotel for lunch. The young cook offered more of the same food we had eaten for breakfast. I skipped the meal, and Mariam and I walked while the others ordered. It was the hottest time of the day, but given how little time we had to explore, we were willing to tolerate the dry heat of Oodweyne.

Many of the traditional adobe homes I remembered were gone. Still, I saw a few that revealed the skills of the old-brick master artisans. Half a century later, the mud bricks were intact.

Signs of modern technology, however, were also visible. A few giant satellite dishes, each guarded by a ring of thorny branches, were dotted about, clearly providing contemporary services to their owners.

We looked for the house where I had lived. The building had undergone a facelift, but no one was home, and we weren't able to have a look inside. The surroundings had changed beyond recognition. The playground and the teachers' home had disappeared entirely.

A woman sat washing clothes in the shade in front of her house on one street. She pretended to look busy, but I noticed her watching us as we approached. When we drew level with her, she spoke.

"Who is this man taking pictures of our ruins?" she asked.

"An old boy from this village," I replied, asserting my claim to the place. She paused to listen to my explanation. I said I wanted the pictures of the old buildings to remember the Oodweyne of my childhood.

"I thought you wanted to embarrass us by showing people the run-down structures of Oodweyne." Then she changed the subject and asked about the start of our journey.

"We left the Gacan Libaax area this morning."

The mention of Gacan Libaax made her sit up. The name gave her the clues she needed to place us.

"Nin Muusa Cabdale ah miyaad tahay?" she asked. *So you're from the Muusa Abdulla sub-clan?*

"Haa," I said. *Yes.* The answer satisfied her. We did indeed have a right to wander through Oodweyne.

My old village had grown and gained the status of a district centre. Oodweyne deserves this recognition, considering its role in the struggle against Barre's regime. Oodweyne was a nodule for the guerrilla members and the network of sympathisers. Barre's army deployed a force to Oodweyne to disrupt SNM activities. Still, the strategy failed because people in the area vigorously supported the rebellion against Barre's dictatorship.

Later in the afternoon, I walked through the town with my brother and MP Guuleed. We set out to find Umal, a second cousin. Our search was easy, and we said goodbye to Umal after chatting for an hour. We then headed on a gravel road for Burco, fifty kilometres east of Oodweyne.

Transit Stop

On the road to Burco is Ceel Xume, a village with a tog. Ceel Xume, I heard, was changing its name from Bad Well to Wholesome Well (Ceel Same) because its fortunes had improved. Ceel Same was now attracting more nomadic herds than in the past.

Already a renowned oasis, Oodweyne had become a district headquarters, but the oasis had to contend with *garanwaa* (*Prosopis juliflora*), an invasive plant of South American origin partly clogging the tributaries of the river's lower reaches.

Past Ceel Same, we entered Aroori, a plain stretching to the horizon. Aroori had good rainfall. The showers had turned the landscape green except for the white spots denoting sheep and goats. Our convoy stopped twice for a break. I used these opportunities to look closely at the ground cover.

I discovered a variety of desert plants in bloom and took pictures. *Wan cad* (white sheep) and *gabal daye* were the only shrubs I recognised. Wan cad is a small shrub with olive-coloured leaves and a cluster of woolly blossoms on each branch tip. I remember people using this material as a filling for pillows.

Gabal daye has soft, greenish leaves and pale-yellow flowers. The leaves and flowers of this shrub follow the sun, hence the Somali name "Admirer of the Sun."

Past Aroori, the change of scenery took us by surprise. The beautiful landscape gave way to clutter as we approached Burco, the second-largest city in Somaliland. There was evidence of massive trash dumping on the outskirts of the town. On arrival, we checked in at a new hotel with a colourful exterior and floors decorated with dark blue floral tiles.

Burco has the biggest livestock market in East Africa. This unassuming town with mostly single-floor buildings has honourable mentions in Somalilanders' struggles against repressive rulers.

In the 1940s, Sheekh Bashir revolted against British rule. The movement unnerved the colonial government, whose memory of Maxamed Cabdile Xasan's twenty-year rebellion was fresh. Ultimately, the British captured Sheekh Bashir and killed him. To this day, people honour Sheekh Bashir.

They also recite Aaden Axmed's poem, lamenting the fall of this local hero. He said,

> Duhur baa Bashiir lagu shanaday daar agtiina ahe,
> Duur looma jabin geesigii dirirta waynaa ye.

> *Bashiir was killed near you in broad daylight.*
> *And no one snapped a twig to avenge the loss of a brave man*
> *who waged war [against the British].*

On another occasion, residents of Burco defied a colonial decision on the taxation of camels reaching Burco's wells. When the British pressed them for payments, tensions increased. A local man took the law into his hands. He fatally wounded Allan Gibb, the British district commissioner of Burco and a veteran of the British campaigns against Sayid Maxamed Cabdile Xasan, who had agitated against British colonialism for two decades.

The colonial authorities demanded the surrender of the assailant, but elders pretended they didn't know him. As punishment, British authorities flew in two Royal Aircraft planes from Aden, Yemen, and bombed the town. They also imposed a fine of 3,000 camels. This payment is equivalent to the traditional compensation for the lives of thirty Somali men. The locals paid the hefty fine instead of surrendering one of their own for standing up against injustice. The incident is notable for another reason. It marked the end of the British drive to increase taxes. In the next three decades, Burco had peace, and its population grew.

While in Burco, I also recalled more recent events in and around the city. In the 1980s, military dictator General Siyaad Barre was the enemy of the people. He oversaw a system that ignored cries for justice, better schools, and health services. Relief came when an SNM force under Colonel Axmed Mire Maxamed captured Burco in 1988.

I recognised one among the officers playing a pivotal role in the offensive: Maxamed Kaahin, the current Minister of Interior of Somaliland. Kaahin was my classmate at the Burco Technical Institute in 1968. I chose the school, thinking it would provide essential background to my goal of becoming an engineer. That interest faded quickly, however. I left the Institute for Sheekh Secondary, a grammar school.

Kaahin and I are also distantly related on the maternal side. I remember him introducing me to his mother in Burco one day in 1968. After completing school, Kaahin joined the Somali Army and trained in a military academy in Odesa in the Soviet Union. Kaahin also played a significant role in the rebellion that ended Barre's draconian rule in Somaliland.

Burco is also the home of Maxamed Ibraahin Warsame (Hadraawi), the most famous living Somali poet, playwright, and song composer. He wrote at least 200 Somali poems. Hadraawi informed and entertained fellow Somalis for decades. His chastisement of Barre's regime earned him punishment. Unable to secure Hadraawi's allegiance, Barre sent the poet to jail for five years. While incarcerated, Hadraawi wrote eight long poems. His poem "Dhallaacan," on resistance to dictatorship, has 700 verses.

"As the stomach needs food, so the brain needs beautiful words," said Hadraawi when asked about poetry. Had it not been for the Poetry Translation Centre in the United Kingdom, non-Somali speakers would not have tasted the wisdom of this sage.

Hadraawi belongs to a handful of men who earned respect and admiration for their unwavering commitment to development, social justice, peace, and reconciliation of factions of Somalis at odds with each other. After the ousting of the Barre regime, Hadraawi returned to Burco to teach at a local university.

Burco's rural life concealed its progressive streak. In the early 1950s, the community hosted the first girls' boarding school in Somaliland. The second boarding school for girls in Somaliland opened decades later in Hargeysa.

My friends and I occasionally travelled from Hargeysa to Sheekh via Burco. The only bus service in Somaliland ran along this route. I believe it was the one that brought me from Isiolo, Kenya, in 1960.

The bus was more comfortable than the truck that frequented the Hargeysa-Berbera-Sheekh route. It was also more memorable for another reason. Girls from the Burco school travelled on the bus in clusters. As teen-agers, we were fully aware of their presence.

We caught the fleeting glances, the shimmer of their silky dresses, the jingles of their bracelets, and the whiffs of their perfume; however, at the end of each journey, we always went our separate ways.

But with Sheekh beckoning on this journey, we didn't linger in Burco. By 9 am the following day, we were back on the tarmac road. The drive was quick. We crossed a landscape with light vegetation, mostly acacia and reddish soil.

Our vehicles on this trip were much better appointed than the lorries we travelled on in the past, with their jarring incessant bumps, dust, and the stink of animals packed on the back.

As we approached Sheekh, I saw familiar landmarks – Dubar Hill and a tog to the south. I had travelled this route many times before. On one of those trips, a relative said: "Madar Yuusuf dooxan agtiisa ayuu ku aasanya-he." *Madar Yuusuf's grave was somewhere near this river.*

Madar Yuusuf was my mother's grandfather. The relative relating the story was Aftax, one of my mother's cousins.

On this journey, we recited verses of the Quran for this ancestor, as was expected.

Then we drove past a fenced area within which several large build-ings had been erected, including some that looked like aircraft hangers. Government property, I presumed.

"This belongs to a sheikh from the Gulf States," our driver said. "He comes here for the mountain air and hunting."

Later, I learnt more about the new interests of Arab sheikhs in this part of the country. What was the draw for wealthy Arabs, I wondered. Solitude? The cooler and clean air?

My brother told me that wealthy Arabs wanted property near Gacan Libaax, but local communities had rejected the foreigners' overtures. I wondered if the camps I drove by belonged to the same man.

Sheekh

Sheekh nested in a rugged terrain. From afar, only the silhouette of the hills loomed large in the background. The town came into view only after we had gotten closer.

Since leaving Burco, we had gained 1,500 metres in altitude. The gain was imperceptible over the sixty-three-kilometre journey, but Sheekh concealed a surprise for any traveller passing through the Sheekh Pass.

We paused at the outskirts of town to allow Guuleed to announce our arrival. He talked with someone on the phone for about ten minutes and said, "Yes, we can go now, but this is not a good time for a visit."

Students were writing their final examinations. The principal wanted peace at the campus, yet he made an exception for us probably because we were graduates of the institution.

We followed an asphalt road to Sheekh Secondary School. Everything looked the same inside the gate though it did not exist in my time. The assembly hall had been readied for students to write their final year examinations. The orderly scene in the hall was identical to what I remembered from my time. Single-person desks stood in straight lines. The desks were sufficiently far apart to thwart any temptation of cheating.

We split into two groups to tour the campus. One group went with my brother Max, who lived in House D between 1964 and 1968. Mariam and Guuleed went with me to House C, where I lodged between 1968 and 1972.

My old dormitory was unchanged. The stonework and walls were intact. Even the colour of the paint on the buildings was the same.

Someone said the school had sustained damages during the civil war. Austrian philanthropist Hermann Gmeiner and his SOS Children's Villages deserve credit for the school's rehabilitation.

Sheekh Secondary School reopened in 2003 after a closure of fifteen years. The significance of this event almost escaped me. The closure meant fifteen cohorts of bright students missed life-changing learning opportunities. This number is larger than the tally of all graduates during the first eleven years of the school's history, between its inception in 1959 and my graduation in 1972. There could have been educators, caregivers, entrepreneurs, and leaders in this lost group.

Since the school's reopening, enrolment has grown from 200 to 250 students in nearly fifty years. In 2019, it had 250 students. About twenty per cent of the students were females. The admission of girls marked the beginning of a new era.

A 2016 video clip I saw on the internet celebrated Sheekh's victory in an international competition. The subject was renewal energy and sustainability. The United Arab Emirates organised the event. The school's solar heating project won the top spot, including a cash prize of USD 100,000. The victory came barely fourteen years after the school's reopening.

The commendable achievement contrasts with the air of decrepitude around the dormitory I visited. Old socks, men's underwear, jeans, and shoes were scattered in the courtyards. The students' tolerance for poor sanitation astonished me. I am sure students from my time hadn't been as lax and sloppy as this!

Unable to view the classrooms, we settled for a quick tour of the dining room and the central courtyard. These sections of the campus looked neat. In the open yard, someone had installed what looked like a statue. By and large, the rest of the campus looked great.

Before leaving, we paused at the staff room. There was not one female teacher in the group.

We thanked the headmaster for letting us visit. Then we drove to our next stop, Sheekh Intermediate School, about two kilometres northeast of Sheekh Secondary. Sheekh Intermediate School was my stepping stone to Sheekh Secondary. My three elder brothers went there before me, as did many leaders of Somaliland.

Halfway to Sheekh Intermediate School, I asked the driver to stop briefly near the old playgrounds. Three of the four fields had disappeared. I wondered if the school had lost its stellar reputation in sports.

Sheekh Intermediate School is now an agricultural college. The administration building and classrooms have undergone rehabilitation; however, the architects have preserved the old look of the place. Two mature acacias stood near the administration building. I took this as a mark of appreciation for these beautiful trees.

We parked in front of an iron gate with a bold picture of the school's mascot. Inspired by the Laas Geel rock paintings, the image of a cow sporting a series of neck rings makes the college stand out. In my time, no school had a mascot.

A guide introduced us to the principal, a well-dressed young man. The principal's idea of a tour was a walk across the renovated campus with stops at places he considered attractive. Our first stop was the depot, where the school extracts butane from raw animal manure. Then we went to the shiny laboratories run by female technicians.

I followed the principal with due appreciation but yearned to visit the old buildings. I peeled off from the group when our host invited us to tea. My brother, niece, and Guuleed joined him. Instead, I went on a separate tour of the old campus with a teacher who had graduated in 1997. Mariam joined me as we ventured into an area of the school that seldom attracted visitors. We squeezed through a bush fence to reach the old section of the campus.

I was disappointed. The only remnants of the old buildings were the door frames, arches, and fireplaces. Hardy shrubs flourished among the ruins. I struggled to get my bearings right. Just then I heard the voice of a woman. I turned and saw a lone figure in a faded dress standing near one of the derelict buildings.

"Are you looking for the old dining rooms?" she asked.

"Yes," I said.

"I'm Jaamac Moogeh's daughter."

The name sounded familiar, but I could not place it right away. Then the fog in my memory cleared. He was the old storekeeper!

She approached us, pointing out one of the ruins.

"This one was Axmed Yare's kitchen," she said. "That one there was Shalakho's. And the one next to it was the canteen."

We stared. Then I turned to Mariam. "Our school had two dining halls – one for School A students and one for School B students. I was in School B, and I spent time out there."

We walked through the ruins without getting snared on hook thorns of acacia.

On the walk, I came upon one standing building that looked familiar. I recognised it instantly. Rhino House! We moved closer, and sure enough, I was right.

Rhino was one of the oldest buildings in the school. It once served as a military dormitory.

"This was my lodging when I arrived here in 1964," I told Mariam.

A thick wall divided the long building into two parts, each section with a door at the far end. The dormitory had four creaky windows. Arranged against the walls in two rows, there were fifty-two beds in this dormitory.

An exuberant growth of vegetation prevented us from getting closer to the building. The bushes, the old building, and the hills to the east set a vivid picture I'll remember for a long time.

We hastened back to the others, avoiding the hooked thorns which have the fitting name *ngoja kidogo* in Kiswahili. This means "wait a moment" in English.

Altogether, Mariam and I felt amply rewarded by the side tour. We thanked the principal and his staff for hosting us. Then we went to our final stop in Sheekh, the old government Guest House.

Sheekh had a government residence known as the Guest House since colonial times. It was a prominent place with luxurious bedrooms, elegant arches, and fireplaces. The reception led to a small garden with stone walls and bougainvillea.

Colonial officials used the place as a retreat during the hot season when coastal temperatures soared to 45 degrees Celsius. After independence, the government of Somalia took over the residence.

The last civilian head of state of Somalia, Cabdirashiid Cali Sharmaarke, and his entourage, including Xaaji Yuusuf Imaan, then the defence minister, spent the night at the Guest House in 1968 or early 1969. Maxamed, Xaaji Yuusuf's eldest son, and I went there to greet our elder. The place was buzzing with dignitaries and military personnel.

The minister came to meet us outside the compound for a moment. But when it was time for Xaaji Yuusuf to return, the security guards at the gate refused him entry. Maxamed and I were speechless, but Xaaji Yuusuf spoke softly to the underlings and waited outside with us until a senior officer came to his aid. Later, the soldiers apologised to their commander-in-chief. I learnt a lesson on leadership that day.

The Guest House had a panoramic view of the hills. About 500 metres to the east, a square, whitewashed tomb gleamed in the sunlight. That was the burial ground of the pious man, Sheekh Qudub, who bestowed his name on the village.

There was open space in the hills leading to the Sheekh Pass to the north and the Golis Mountains to the west.

The Guest House was derelict. Nothing of the old charm had survived except the views. The roof was gone, and the walls had collapsed. What remained were arches, fireplaces, and cracked floors. Wild shrubs claimed the garden. Even the hardy eucalyptus trees looked gnarled. The concrete tennis court served as a parking lot.

I wondered whether the charming bungalows in the western valley had survived. They had not. The stonework of the fireplaces and chimneys were the only reminders that they'd once existed.

We swung by the old post office on our way out of the area. The place holds an unforgettable memory for me. It was here that I picked up a telegram from my mother in 1970.

"AABO IS VERY ILL STOP COME HOME AS SOON AS POSSIBLE STOP HOYO."

This telegram was the only written message I ever received from my mother, and I acted on it. I left Sheekh on a truck to Hargeysa via Berbera that same day. I made it to Hargeysa in less than twelve hours. Aabo died two weeks later.

The old post office building had a gaping roof, shuttered door, and thoroughly washed-out paint. All the other buildings near it looked un-inhabitable. Barre's government sent some of the Sheekh residents to the Mandheera Prison. Others guided SNM members through the mountain trails or provided intelligence, food, and care for wounded fighters.

Under British rule, Sheekh was also a refuge for colonial administrators fleeing the sweltering heat of Berbera during the hot season. Long before the arrival of the British and Maxamed Cabdile Xasan, Sheekh was the abode of Islamic scholars. I saw pilgrims in town during my school days.

In 1964, Sheekh earned yet another accolade. It became a major medical referral centre in the northern part of the Somali Republic after the Somali government, with aid from the Soviet Union, built a large, modern hospital.

My first visit to this village was in 1964. I was a ten-year-old boy uncertain about life in a boarding school. Sheekh taught me nearly everything I knew about the world outside the Somali Republic – from geography to history, algebra to biology, and Arabic. And thanks to my dedicated teachers.

I had Somali and a few Egyptian and American teachers in middle school. The Americans were Peace Corps volunteers. The Egyptians were President Jamal Abdel Nasser's equivalent of the Peace Corps.

Our teachers at the secondary school were British, Indian, and Somali. Darlington, an Englishman, was one of the most famous of the lot. This Cambridge graduate landed in British Somaliland during World War II. After the war, he became the founding principal of the colony's first intermediate and secondary schools.

When I started secondary school, Darlington was a tall, slender, clean-shaven man in his fifties. He stood out in any crowd because of his looks, especially his long nose and uniform.

He wore khaki shorts, a white cotton shirt with short sleeves, safari shoes, and white knee-high stockings during working hours. A pipe dangled from his mouth as he walked between his residence and the class-room a few hundred metres apart. The sweet scent of tobacco smoke on the trail was the telltale sign of the man. After hours, Darlington retreated to his residence, but on rare occasions, he returned to his office in the evening dressed in long pants, a tie, and a jacket. And, of course, a pipe in his mouth.

Locals knew him as *Gacma Dheere*, the Somali word for the man with long arms. Gacma Dheere earned the respect of the locals, and for over twenty years, he instructed hundreds of bright students in Amoud and Sheekh, including many of the country's leaders. He taught four members of my family – my elder brothers Xasan, Xuseen, and Maxamuud – and me.

"You have Xuseen's handwriting," he told me on my first day in his English class. "You should live in House D as your brothers did."

I was all smiles. Xuseen was my hero. Darlington did not know the impact of his statement. The mention of a trait I shared with this man was the highest compliment my teacher could have given me, but his suggestion on residence came too late. The new principal, Axmed Sheekh Aaden, had assigned me to House C.

Darlington knew the full names of every student in our schools. I corresponded with him occasionally after high school.

In one letter he said: "I heard from several of the old boys, but I have one letter and I'm afraid I don't recall the face of the sender. Please don't tell him that if you write to him."

My teacher had no reason to worry. I, too, didn't remember the author of the letter.

Darlington and two other British teachers left Somalia in 1972, the same year I graduated from Sheekh Secondary. He died in 2007 at eighty-eight, bequeathing his estate to Cambridge University to finance the education of Somali children.

Sheekh town had a close-knit community. The most influential members were the residents of Dariiqa, a village about five kilometres northwest of the business centre. They promoted education and granted land to the British to build the Sheekh schools.

The school and the Guest House tours lasted roughly half a day. I felt sad about the state of the nation's oldest and finest schools and its government residency.

My thoughts drifted from the ruins in Sheekh to the old institutions I had seen elsewhere. The Al-Azhar University in Cairo was over 1,000 years old when I visited it. Egyptians of different political orientations had come and gone, but the Al-Azhar survived through all the political changes.

Sheekh schools regressed, however, and much of the rot occurred during the tenure of one leader, General Barre. He saw Northerners as a threat and their schools as a breeding ground for troublemakers. He starved the institutions. He even jailed those who worked voluntarily to arrest the decay in the health and education sectors.

The worst treatment came in the 1980s. Barre's forces turned some campuses into temporary troop camps from which they launched attacks on locals.

The decay of Sheekh's historical sites saddened me; however, the rehabilitation of two institutions gave me reasons to hope for what is achievable with little aid. I ended my visit thinking that Sheekh could regain the paramount role it once played in youth education. Sheekh is not only an accessible place, but it also has an impressive record of hosting thousands of students from all over Somaliland.

Sheekh Pass

After a quick tour of local sites, we set off for Berbera, seventy-two kilometres north of Sheekh. This part of the journey started with a short but dramatic downhill drive and a longer ride through a hot and hazy landscape. We dropped 1,500 metres in fourteen kilometres.

The windy Sheekh Pass cuts through a mountain range just north of Sheekh on its way to the port city of Berbera. Britain carved out this pass using Italian prisoners during World War II.

A crossing of the Sheekh Pass was always a scary event, but now, the road was broader, smoother, and safer than in my youth. Civil engineers had reduced the number of hairpin twists and turns. They also laid concrete.

Nevertheless, the hills are steep, the turns sharp, and the drop precipitous. We saw signboards with Islamic prayers along the route. People usually recite these expressions of faith when confronted with the imminent prospect of death.

Our driver cautiously put the Toyota Land Cruiser in second gear for the descent. The engine groaned. The change of sound prompted me to comment.

"At this speed, our descent will take a long time." The comment startled the driver. Immediately, he switched to a higher gear, allowing the vehicle to coast downhill while applying gentle pressure on the brakes at sharp turns.

In no time, we had safely negotiated the infamous Sheekh Pass. Many travellers who have taken this route have stories to tell about it. I shared two such tales with my daughter and niece.

Once, long ago, we hiked to our school from Huduse, the mandatory overnight truck stop for traffic from Berbera. Our incentive was dormitory beds fourteen kilometres away. The moon was bright that night, so we decided to hike to the campus.

The event was memorable for two reasons. First, it was a new experience. Second, the Somali Army toppled the civilian government during our hike. I learnt of the coup d'état around 10 am the next day when I heard martial music pouring out of a short-wave radio in my dormitory.

I also shared the tale of a driver whose truck plunged down a ravine. The man, a relative, sustained multiple fractures, but he miraculously survived and returned to his job after years of physical rehabilitation. In my family circle, he was the living reminder of the perils of the Sheekh Pass.

Huduse, the village at the bottom of the pass, prompted another story about straw beds and bone-chilling winds sweeping down the hills. All night travellers spent hours in the town because the Sheekh Pass closed until dawn. A howling wind made the wait unbearably long.

For bedding, we had a choice. We could rent straw beds, which would cost us a few shillings, or slumber on sacks of sugar or rice, the usual cargo.

Once, I snuggled under a tarpaulin sheet. It was warmer there but stuffier. Every driver had one to protect their precious cargo from sudden downpours.

My one experiment with the straw beds left me a few shillings poorer and colder because the wind hit me from above and below. The fee for that bed was about one-third of my weekly stipend in secondary school.

My daughter and niece listened to my tales of the old days until we crossed the pass.

Ahead of us lay the Guban zone, forty kilometres of treeless plain baked by a relentless sun. How the scattered scrub survived, I don't know.

The burnt-out landscape (*Guban* means "burnt" in Somali) stretched north to the Red Sea. The closer we got to Berbera, the scantier the vegetation. We passed a lone gravel facility in the hills outside Berbera. Its machinery chewed the rocks to supply gravel for Berbera's thriving construction industry.

Berbera

At Berbera, my smartphone's weather application blinked red. The temperature was 45 degrees Celsius. At that moment, I realised our mistake. We did not heed the general advisory that says travellers should stay away if they can't bear the heat.

My daughter and I made the trip in June because this was convenient for both of us. Furthermore, June was a pleasant time to travel to other stops on our itinerary. The tail end of the monsoon season made this arid land bloom. But I forgot the Berbera microclimate. Perhaps I was too excited about the trip.

Indeed, our timing was off. We entered Berbera at 1 pm, the hottest hour of the day. The streets were empty, and the sky was grey. Even the coastal birds had sought shelter in cooler climates, or they would have risked heat stroke in flight.

On arrival, I rolled down the window of the moving car. A blast of air, hotter than the emission of a blow dryer, gushed in. Only age saved me from a reprimand from my daughter and niece. I promptly closed the window.

We followed the lead car to Mansoor Hotel, a tree-lined beachfront property in Batalaale. In front of us was a ring of dhamas (*Conocarpus lancifolius*) trees shading the concrete wall and the main hotel parking area. Behind us, I saw the glare of the beach sand and, beyond it, a sliver of Red Sea water.

I shuffled my feet past the guard post to the restaurant where split air conditioning (AC) units were humming, but I felt no relief. A young waiter took pity on our group. He ushered us into another room, a hall with curtains shutting off the light and humming with more AC units. Here, at last, we felt relief. Only then did we think of food.

There was no menu. A young waiter in black trousers and a white shirt announced the offerings.

"Hilib adhi, hilib geel, bariis, baasto, iyo kaluun," he said. *Goat meat. Camel meat. Rice. Pasta and fish.*

As an afterthought, he mentioned the drinks: freshly squeezed watermelon, papaya, and melon juice.

In the past, people seldom ate seafood. The waiter's mention of fish signalled to me that there had been a change in the diet. Still, I doubted if our waiter could differentiate the varieties of seafood on offer.

"How is the fish prepared?" I asked.

He thought for a moment, trying to compose a response. "Basically," he said, "we have dry fish and wet fish."

"Wet fish and rice for me," I said. "Dessert?"

"Fruits."

The ACs groaned, reminding me of our Land Cruiser in second gear when it was coming down the Sheekh Pass. We hoped the cooling motor would hold out until we'd finished our meal.

After lunch, Guuleed introduced us to Cabdi Shakur Maxamuud, the young mayor of Berbera. Cabdi Shakur is a second cousin on my mother's side.

We talked briefly about our families in Somaliland and Kenya. Then the mayor left. Guuleed, the member of Parliament who had been travelling with us since Go'da Weyn, decided to stay behind in Berbera. Our driver went out for a dip in the sea while I sought a place to hide.

Under the shadow of one AC unit, I pulled four chairs side by side like a bed and lay in the dining hall. A waiter jerked me out of a fitful doze by telling me the hotel needed the reception room. We set off in search of an alternative.

He took us to another room with a few AC units. I slumped there until another waiter jolted me out of my stupor.

"We need this room," he said.

My brother announced that it was still too hot to travel. We had to find another shelter for a bit longer.

We arranged chairs in the shade near the reception and ordered refreshments. While some party members chose cold drinks, I asked for hot tea, hoping the caffeine would give me a boost.

By the time we finished our tea, the temperature had dropped a few degrees. I felt better.

We left the hotel around 4 pm, picking up a middle-aged man on our way out of town. He joined my daughter and niece in the back seat. The driver explained that he was the local agent of our car hire company.

The car stopped again at a gas station. An attendant promptly went to work. Then the man who hitched the ride in our vehicle punched numbers on his smartphone to effect payment. No cash changed hands, and there were no credit cards either!

The electronic transaction was dreamlike. It gave me a deeper appreciation for the work of private institutions that did not exist when I last visited Somaliland in 1984. Cell phones (Telesom and Somtel) and money transfer companies (Dahabshiil and WorldRemit) have changed the landscape. Now Somaliland has fast and reliable channels of money transfer.

We set off for Hargeysa, which offered relief from the oppressive heat of Berbera. An hour before entering the city, Nasa Hablood came into view. The famous conical hills stood against the setting sun. A light shower swept through the area just before we entered the town at dusk.

Suddenly, the change of scenery sparked a reflection on Berbera. I blamed the June heat for my excessive lamentation about the city.

Berbera is more than a hot place. It is one of the oldest towns on the Red Sea coast. Arab, Indian, Jewish, and Somali merchants once mingled there. People traded coffee, frankincense, myrrh, acacia gum, saffron, feathers, wax, ghee, hides, and ivory.

In the cool months of the year, October to April, Berbera once held an annual trade fair that attracted thousands of people. More than 6,000 camels laden with goods arrived daily from the interior. By one estimate, the town's population swelled to 70,000 in 1833.

Charles Xavier Rochet d'Héricourt, a French explorer, described Berbera as "the freest port in the world and the most important place in the whole of the Arabian Gulf."

Another European wrote, "Berbera was the true key of the Red Sea, the centre of East African traffic and the only safe place for shipping upon the western Erythraean shore from Suez to Gardafui."

Aden, a seaport lying 260 kilometres to the north, once relied heavily on tax revenues on goods imported from Berbera. In 1848, the imports generated eighty per cent of Aden's revenue.

Berbera came under Ottoman occupation in 1546. Then Britain took it over in 1884, turning this possession into the capital of the Somaliland Protectorate until 1941.

Berbera's importance has not diminished. Today, it is a thriving trade centre and the capital of the Sahel region. The strategic and economic prominence of the town is rising for two reasons. One is the ongoing expansion of the facilities of the deep port. The other is the Berbera airport. It has a runway fit for combat aircraft and other aircraft requiring long runways. The US government once designated it as a secondary landing site for the space shuttle in case of an emergency.

Visits

Mariam and I needed at least a day of rest in Hargeysa after the whirlwind trip to Gacan Libaax, Go'da Weyn, Oodweyne, Burco, Sheekh, and Berbera.

At Masalaha in Hargeysa, we again appreciated the convenience of reading lights, hot showers on demand, flush toilets, excellent meals, a breezy veranda, and a small garden.

My head spun, however, with thoughts on the Go'da Weyn cemetery, my schools, and my ancestral village.

As a first-time visitor to Somaliland and a non-speaker of the local language, Mariam managed situations admirably. She retained much information while her politeness, curiosity, and lack of complaints impressed the people we met.

At Gacan Libaax, her agility surprised the men who presumed the cave trail would challenge our women. And, despite the language barrier, she found ways to engage with children and put a smile on their faces.

One day, the five-year-old son of my nephew, Ibraahin, commented on her manner of speaking. He noticed that she only used short phrases.

"Eddo, Somali run ah ku hadal," he said. *Auntie, speak real Somali.*

We translated the remark, and Mariam smiled at the child's observations. Meanwhile, his baby sister had another idea. She crawled onto Mariam's lap.

My brother and sister, Amina, prepared traditional Somali feasts for us. We started with the banquet at Max and his wife Nuura's home near the Maxamed Moogeh neighbourhood. There, I met their only daughter, Bushra, who always wore a bashful smile.

At this reception, I met up with Siciid Foodcade, a relative I had not seen for forty-seven years. Siciid was a young nurse in the Hargeysa Tuberculosis Hospital in the 1960s. He had a hand in my treatment there.

I sought care for a recurring cough when I was schooling in Oodweyne. The Indian doctor at the hospital ordered a chest X-ray and a sputum test. Both were negative, but he recommended a month's treatment with antibiotic injections and other drugs whose names I do not remember. Siciid made sure that I completed the treatment. The doctor did not explain the purpose of the treatment, and, like most patients, I did not ask questions.

In 2005, a French doctor at the SOS Hospital in Hanoi, Vietnam, where I worked, told me that I had minor scarring on one of my lungs. The finding during a routine medical examination reminded me of Siciid and the Indian physician at the Hargeysa hospital. The information surprised me because no one had mentioned it previously although I had that scarring over twelve routine medical examinations.

Intrigued by the SOS doctor's findings in Hanoi, I sought a second opinion at the Bumrungrad, a top-notch hospital in Bangkok. A physician there confirmed the French doctor's diagnosis. "But this is nothing of consequence," he said.

In Hargeysa, I thanked Siciid for the help he'd given me with my treatment as a child. He hugged me but did not seem interested in a medical matter that had played out over half a century ago. I followed his lead and focused on the reunion.

Amina's feast took place on her farm, a fifty-acre property near Sheekh Aw Barkhadleh. The site has small hills on one side and a tog on the other. A dirt track connected it to the Hargeysa-Berbera Road.

"Stay on the track marked with rocks painted blue," Maxamed, one of Amina's sons, told us.

He explained that the farm sits twenty kilometres north of the tank base in northern Somalia. Fearing attacks from SNM guerrillas, Siyaad Barre's regime planted landmines on the approaches to the base in the late 1980s. Stones coloured bright blue now demarcated the only safe path through the mines.

Amina's farm near Aw Barkhadleh was as thirsty for water as Max's near Go'da Weyn. Undeterred by water scarcity, Amina had planted trees of various kinds and built one rustic cabin. She uses the place as a retreat from the hustle and bustle of Hargeysa.

There, we had another Somali feast under a large tree on the bank of the tog.

When the schedule of visits became hectic, I took advantage of the privilege of age. I sorted relatives into two groups: those older than me and those younger.

"Adeer, da'ada yaryari halkan ha igu timaado," I said. *The younger relatives can visit me here.*

I'd make the trip to the homes of the older group.

Raxma, a grandniece, responded to my call. She gathered members of her family and showed up at our residence. Raxma is a British citizen and one of the relatives who sought refuge in the United Kingdom during the war.

"I am working with the United Nations Development Programme (UNDP) in Hargeysa," she told me.

Two nephews who had just completed their secondary school education in Hargeysa also visited. One fellow was talkative, the other reserved.

"Adeer, inaanu jaamicado galno ayaanu rabnaa," they said. *Uncle, we want a university education.*

The eagerness was palpable in their voices. The more effusive nephew had set his eyes on schools in foreign countries.

"Waad dadaasheen," I said. *You worked hard.*

Then I suggested we wait for the secondary school examination outcome before we plunged into a more in-depth conversation on university education and financing.

On another occasion, I visited another second cousin, Sahra, who was like a sister to me. Her mother, Xaajia Faadumo, took care of me as a youngster.

Sahra had worked with the UN agencies and has now retired. She embraced her father's value for education and has helped others. One such individual was a niece who studied architecture, making this young woman the first member of our extended family to venture into this field.

After the visit with Sahra, we popped into the house of another young relative who had just returned from Holland. The young man wore a scruffy beard, a white kanzu, a hat, sandals, and a scarf with reddish stripes. I asked about his plans.

"Caruurtaa ayaan keeney halkan si ay quraanka ubartaan," he said. *I brought the young children here to attend the Islamic school and learn the Quran.*

I didn't ask what the plan was after the summer holidays.

In Hargeysa, I crossed paths with people with ties to Europe, North America, the Middle East, and East Africa. It was rare to see such a network of families before the civil war. The most common traveller in the old days was a pilgrim from Mecca, an oil industry employee, or a student.

Night Out

"Do you want to visit the Hiddo Dhawr?" asked my second cousin, Saamiya. Hiddo Dhawr is a cultural centre that offers live music performances at night.

"Yes," I said, curious about nightlife in Hargeysa and keen to expose Mariam to live music. I yearned for the days when Hargeysa's Freedom Garden, then a green place, came alive with colourful lights and loud-speakers whenever there was a play, and plays always included songs. The Freedom Garden featured Sudanese singers, such as Maxamed Al Wardi, Sayid Al Khalifa, and Cabdulkarim Al Kabili, when they were touring.

I set out at 7 pm in the company of four young women – my daughter, two nieces, and one of their female friends.

There were many cars in the parking area when we reached the place. A young fellow directed us to the drop-off point where we met armed security guards. They checked handbags, collected the tickets, and led us to our next stop.

We walked past a building, which had a display of traditional artefacts. Ushers then led us to a table that Saamiya had reserved for us. Guests were already having their dinner. We sat about two-thirds back from the stage.

Everyone was young, no more than thirty-five years old. The men wore tight-fitting pants and jackets. The young women came in colourful kaftans and silky scarves. The jingles of gold bracelets adorning their arms and laughter filled the air. I felt out of place.

Young male servers darted from one table to another carrying large trays with plates loaded with food and soft drinks. Dinner was rice with chicken stew or a pasta dish with minced meat sauce. The drinks – cans of Coke and Sprite and bottled water – were wet with condensation. These offerings were free, but there was no dessert, coffee, or tea. Loudspeakers pulsed with Somali music all during dinner.

Around 9 pm, a woman dressed much like the young women patrons appeared on stage with a microphone.

"That woman is Sahra Halgan, the owner," said Saamiya.

Sahra, I heard, had a deep interest in promoting Somali culture. She is a veteran of the SNM, which she joined as a nurse at a young age.

Sahra greeted everyone in Somali.

"Hablaha waxyar baan u sheegayaa," she said. "Waad quruxsantihiin. Mashaa Allah. Laakinse wax yar baan idinka codsanayaa. Walaal timihiina daboola si aynu sharciga ula socono. Waad mahadsantihiin. Madadaaladuna dakhso ayey inoogu bilaabmeysaa." *Girls, you look beautiful. God bless. But I ask you to cover your hair to follow the rules. Thank you. The entertainment will begin shortly.*

I presumed "rules" meant a government-sponsored dress code. Then Sahra sang the first song of the evening, and the audience applauded. The song's love theme still held sway, but the entertainment style had markedly changed. An electronic keyboard, which I didn't care much for, had gained popularity.

A man in a grey suit followed. He walked from table to table with a hand-held microphone, taunting the audience to sing along. I shook my head no when he paused at our table. He moved on to another one where he found more willing clients. This routine lasted almost twenty minutes before giving way to our hostess. She sang two Somali songs I did not know. The crowd applauded.

The cycle of songs repeated. By 11 pm, we had heard enough and were ready to leave. The singing and applause got softer as we walked to the car. We said good night to the two guardsmen with guns and boarded our vehicle.

The night traffic was light, and we reached home quickly after making two stops. There were no policemen in sight.

"Adeer, it is safe here. Very safe," said Saamiya. "You should see the place during Ramadan. People stay up late. Women and children walk about without fear. Once, I left a wedding party late on another occasion and drove home alone. I opened the metal gate and let myself into the empty house. I had no worries."

I cringed at the thought of my female cousin driving late at night in many other African or North American cities.

The outing in Hargeysa cost USD 15 per person. The fee covered the entertainment and dinner. The new songs did not win me over, but I enjoyed the excursion and will never forget the feeling of security in an unfamiliar city.

Hiddo Dhawr offered the youth a rare venue for social interaction. It also promoted Somali music, an essential medium of expression. Indeed, songs played a vital role in the struggle against the dictatorship of General Barre. Had I met the owner, Sahra Halgan, I'd have saluted her for the initiative at Hiddo Dhawr.

Borama

The first part of our tour to Somaliland was over, but I still had other relatives to visit, so we were back on the road again. Our next destination was Borama, the capital of the Awdal region, 100 kilometres west of Hargeysa. In the 1960s, such a car trip took at least three hours. A much-improved road now reduced the travel time to about an hour.

Borama had escaped the wrath of Siyaad Barre's armies. I wondered how it had weathered the years. I also wanted Mariam to meet relatives there and visit Amoud University, a primary source of Western education in Somaliland.

A relatively higher rainfall pattern fostered subsistence farming west of Hargeysa; however, the importance of agriculture appeared to be declining. A friend in New York City who grew up in Gebiiley told me that reduced rainfall had frustrated traditional farmers. If this trend continues, local food production will drop, forcing farmers to find a new vocation.

The route between Hargeysa and Borama boasted more villages than that between Berbera and Hargeysa; however, area residents were counting on the Berbera-Tog Wajaale road to create new opportunities for trade and commerce.

As we approached the turn-off to Gebiiley, a grove of eucalyptus trees came into view. This section of road was like no other. It had trees on both sides. The slender grey trunks and the shimmer of the silvery leaves were refreshing in a country where the vegetation is sparse and thorny. I shouted out to the diligent farmers who planted them decades ago.

At the eastern outskirts of Borama, I pointed out Goroyo Cawl to my daughter and niece. This village was a base for a commando battalion of the Somali National Army. I knew about it through my brother, Xuseen Dheere, who lived there when I was in high school. I spent one summer holiday with him at the camp.

Goroyo Cawl lost its strategic importance with the return of peace between Somaliland and Ethiopia. I heard it was popular with people seeking affordable plots around Borama.

I called Maxamed, my brother Xuseen's oldest son, to alert him of our arrival.

"Maxamed, where shall we meet?"

"Uncle, find a place to stop. Then call me."

Nuura suggested we go to the Oslo Hotel in the centre of town. The parking was full, so we left the car on the street with all our bags, including my camera gear, and walked to the hotel. Only male clients lounged at the tables under the shade in the courtyard. Our party had two young women. The waiter noted this and seated us in a shed with large windows, a safe space from prying eyes. Presently, my nephew and his maternal uncle, Cabdillaahi, joined us.

Cabdillaahi proposed a quick tour of the town and Amoud University campus before we visited their homes. We liked the idea. Six of us piled into one vehicle and drove to a hilltop with a panoramic view. Borama lay below us in the midday haze.

The small green town I'd explored in 1969 had become a sprawling city. Hundreds of buildings lay before us, including many with shiny corrugated roofs. Rubbish, the curse of urbanisation, littered the streets. Amoud University, the next stop on our tour, sat in the eastern quadrant of Borama. On our way to Amoud, Cabdillaahi pointed out a cluster of pinkish buildings.

"The President's Residence," he said.

Hyatt Hospital stood on the opposite side of the road. This facility, which post-dates my last visit to Borama, had developed a reputation for providing high-quality medical care.

We entered a wooded area and drove for ten minutes before seeing any buildings.

"We've arrived," said Cabdillaahi, a former student at this school.

He then gave us a quick tour.

Amoud was once a British military camp. In 1952, the British turned it into a secondary school, the first of its kind in the Somaliland Protectorate. Amoud has since transformed itself from a rival of Sheekh Secondary School to the most reputable university in Somaliland in its latest mutation. It is also the home to the first medical school in the country.

My two eldest brothers, Xasan and Xuseen, started secondary education in Amoud, but neither of them completed their studies there. I recall Xasan, my eldest brother, telling me that his group was moved from Amoud to Sheekh Secondary when it opened in 1959.

Xuseen's ties to the region extended beyond his school years. Returning as an officer, he married the daughter of a prominent Borama family. He once served as mayor of the town. Maxamed is the first offspring of this union. Cabdillaahi is a brother-in-law.

To this day, Amoud has the unmistakable feel of a military camp. It is in a secluded area amidst a beautiful forest of acacia trees.

At about 1 pm, we returned to Borama. We continued to Cabdillaahi's house to greet his mother, Maxamed's grandmother. A few minutes later, Cabdillaahi's sister came to greet us.

"Auntie is looking after Grandma," Maxamed said.

This comment confirmed a conclusion I had drawn from other home visits in Hargeysa. Daughters were the primary caregivers of aged parents.

I introduced my daughter and niece. The auntie stepped out momentarily and returned, pushing her mother in a wheelchair.

The mother greeted me warmly. She asked about the rest of my family. She looked good and was curious about where I had lived these past years. Occasionally, a family member helped if she couldn't remember a name.

She was one of the two oldest members of my extended family still living in Somaliland, and both had a daughter as the caregiver.

Finally, we reached Maxamed's house where we met his wife and three children. Lunch was ready and enjoyable.

Maxamed's son and two daughters had adopted Mariam as an aunt. They crowded around her, talking and laughing.

Then the phone rang. Maxamed answered it. Moments later, he handed it to me and said, "Waa Hooyo." *Mother*, meaning his mother, was on the phone.

I chatted with my sister-in-law and with Kaltuun, her second daughter. Calling from the United Kingdom, they were pleased to learn about our visit to Borama. I had not seen Kaltuun since September 11, 2001. That morning, I had bidden her farewell at the New Rochelle train station in New York about an hour before the first terrorist plane struck the World Trade Center buildings.

In Borama, too, Maxamed was at ease with his new role as a parent. After leaving Mariam's side, one of the kids sat on his lap, and two others interrupted him often with questions intended for us.

The scene brought back memories of our first encounter in 1982. Maxamed was a toddler living with his parents in Luuq, a town in the southwestern corner of Somalia where the Ethiopian-Somali borders meet. His father was the local military commander of the Somali Army. I worked at a refugee camp about forty-five kilometres south of Luuq as the crow flies and about the same distance from Garba Haarey, Siyaad Barre's ancestral town.

En route to Mogadishu, I briefly stopped at the military camp to greet my brother and his family. I met Maxamed and his elder sister, Ayaan, the only children in the household. I have a photo of him wearing flip-flops, khaki shorts, and a T-shirt. A beige officer's beret covered his head to his eyebrows and ears. Maxamed walked about as if he ran the camp. Entertained, the soldiers gave him ample space to perform.

Today, Maxamed would be more comfortable in Borama (his maternal home) and Holland (his new home) than Luuq, the town his father once protected from Ethiopian incursions. Maxamed's challenge is his lineage. He belongs to one of the clans that vigorously opposed General Barre's brutal regime.

At 4 pm, we thanked everyone, especially Cabdillaahi, who had spent the day with us, and Maxamed's wife, who had fed us well, and we set off for Hargeysa. At Kalabaydh, we swung by Tog Wajaale, a town on the Somaliland-Ethiopian border. The countryside was flat and treeless, the soil loamy and dark. Fresh grass covered the landscape, and small herds of sheep, cows, and donkeys grazed in the soft afternoon light. I was surprised to see livestock grazing on the land I thought would have been under cultivation.

Tog Wajaale was once the site of a national agricultural experiment. The Soviets had selected the area for wheat farming. The project relied on Soviet experts and heavy equipment not seen in this part of the world.

I remember hearing that Tog Wajaale would become a food basket, but the hopes and dreams of the project quickly faded. In less than a decade, the Soviet-funded project folded. To this day, I don't know what happened. Did the project run out of funding? Did the weather fail them? Did the experts miscalculate?

I had visited the area once before. That was in 1984, and what I saw surprised me. Dead Soviet machinery littered the fields. More alarmingly, dozens of rusty drums were oozing chemicals into the soil.

Tog Wajaale, however, has regained visibility primarily because of the growing trade between Ethiopia and Somaliland. We drove aimlessly on the main street, hoping to catch glimpses of the new life. We were not disappointed.

Hundreds of trucks, hawkers, and pedestrians jammed the street. We could hardly find a parking space near the road. By then, we had driven deep into town to the gulley near the Somaliland-Ethiopian border. Sadly, this no-man's land was not a pretty site. It looked like a dumping ground for trash from both sides of the border. Trading and littering went on side by side in Tog Wajaale.

We cut our tour short and headed east to Hargeysa. In no time, we were back driving through a clean, green countryside until we reached the Borama-Hargeysa Road. We arrived at Hargeysa at dusk, pleased to have seen other relatives in Western Somaliland.

Reunion

With many travels under our belt, I found more time to see old friends and ponder my observations. I visited Dr Diiriye Ismaciil Ereg one day at the Hargeysa University Medical School.

Dr Diiriye was my classmate for eight years in Sheekh and one of the first graduates of the Somali National Medical University in Mogadishu. He completed his post-graduate studies in Turkey and returned to Somalia. After a few years of national service, Dr Diiriye joined the youth fleeing Siyaad Barre's repression.

He worked in Saudi Arabia for a decade. Meanwhile, the situation in Somalia worsened. The quality of education and health services declined. In the North, the frequency of random arrests and imprisonments increased.

In 1994, Dr Diiriye left his well-paying job for Somaliland. He landed in Hargeysa with a wife and two children.

"The situation was bad," he told me. "People were dying from gun injuries and preventable diseases."

Dr Diiriye tended to the sick and wounded. He saved lives and collaborated with fellow physicians to address the shortage of trained personnel. The group founded the Hargeysa Medical University.

Thirty years on, Dr Diiriye was still at it. As the only dean of the school since its inception, he mentors new talent. The school graduated its first crop of fifteen doctors in 2009. By 2021, the tally of graduates had increased to 272. Somalia did not have that many physicians when Dr Diiriye and I were at Sheekh.

I had not seen information on government subventions to the school, but the evidence of strain was palpable. The dean shared an office with two other faculty members – the associate dean and a female graduate who had completed post-graduate studies at the University of Oslo in 2019. Yet, the cramped space was the last thing on the dean's mind when he talked to me about the school and its growing network.

"We have a good relationship with several European universities. Our external examiners come from there," he said with a glint of pride in his eyes.

A moment later, he switched to another subject: the opportunities that his students had for further study outside Somaliland.

"One of our bright graduates is at the University of Cape Town for post-graduate work. Check him out when you return to Southern Africa," he added.

Dr Diiriye is a slender fellow with curly grey hair and spectacles. These features, a tie dangling from his collar or a stethoscope on his shoulder, gave him the aura of the lovable family physician. He lived in a small house in Hargeysa where the elite owned mansions. He navigated the streets in his second-hand Hyundai, undeterred by the elegant SUVs of wealthy residents.

"You can't push your way into Dr Diiriye's school," a student told me. "No way. You have to follow the rules!"

His children attended local universities. One of them is following in his father's footsteps in medicine. Dr Diiriye and others like him are the unsung heroes of Somaliland.

Such men and women have laboured in advancing social causes with few material rewards. The only shreds of appreciation or honour bestowed to him sat in a tall, dark cupboard in the corner of his shared office. I resisted asking Dr Diiriye to tell me the story behind each award. Knowing that he would deflect attention, I let it go. But I snapped a photo of the cupboard and its precious contents for later inspection.

There were two certificates from his old schools: the university in Mogadishu and the Turkish university where he did his specialisation. There were also ten plaques and awards from the University of Hargeysa. The school appreciated Dr Diiriye's teaching, mentoring, and leadership. My favourite tribute is the one that read, "You truly did the impossible."

I thought that the likes of Dr Diiriye made good role models for the young people of Somaliland. He showed them how competence, integrity, and service could coexist.

After we visited Dr Diiriye, Mariam and I spent time with two dozen fourth-year medical students. The young people sat in groups separated by sex: male students on one side and female students on the other. The young men wore casual clothes. None wore T-shirts, baseball caps, or tattoos. But every young woman had a hijab. My daughter and niece, in hijabs, too, sat with them.

I introduced myself as Dr Diiriye's classmate and a retired public health specialist. "I came to see your school," I said.

My introduction elicited fidgeting. I prodded the group until questions came, first from the boys.

"What can you say about the disposal of medical waste?" was the first question.

Then more.

"How do you publish articles in international journals?"

"Why do development agencies support interventions with limited geographic coverage?"

"What have you done for Somaliland?"

Regarding the disposal of medical waste, I used their question as an excuse to talk about urban sanitation in Somaliland. I watched for reactions. No comments came. A few nodded. Others remained impassive. I wasn't sure whether they had become accustomed to littering and could not see it.

I mentioned the child immunisation programme, which addresses the waste it generates. The vaccines come with syringes, needles, and incinerator boxes. Each box produces enough heat to destroy the spent needles and syringes if set on fire.

I recommended that the students familiarise themselves with the guidelines of various journals if they wanted to publish. I also stressed the importance of generating material of interest to the specific journal and its readers. I suggested they use reliable data to make country comparisons.

On contributions to Somaliland, I said, "Nothing." This response elicited silence and gaping mouths.

I considered other responses but gave up the idea after weighing my efforts against the sacrifices of others.

"What is your *dardaaran*?" one fellow asked. Dardaaran is the last word of an elder, parent, or grandparent when parting. A dardaaran has finality to it.

I paused to gather my thoughts. Then I said, "Protect Somaliland's remarkable achievements. Be advocates of peace and security, the environment, and the public goods, *danta guud* in Somali." I hoped a short answer would be more memorable than a long one.

•••

One morning I had coffee with Maxamed Baaruud, a schoolmate, a bright star, and a phenomenal soccer player in our secondary school. Maxamed is a tall fellow with an athletic build. He looked youthful almost fifty years later, except for the receding hairline and a short, greying goatee. We sipped a cappuccino and chatted at his office.

Upon graduation in 1971, Baaruud won one of the few coveted scholarships to the UK. He completed his studies in chemistry and geology and returned to Somalia.

Barre's regime arrested him late one night. He was one of the twenty-eight young men accused of treason. The accused were local youth concerned about the decay of social services under the military government. They approached the business community, NGOs, and Somalilanders in the Gulf States and used aid from these resources to improve the services of Hargeysa Hospital and schools.

This is how Dr Adan Yusuf Abokor, the director of the Hargeysa Hospital, described the initiative that earned him a thirty-year jail term in a maximum-security prison.

[W]e mobilised ourselves and mobilised those people to help me to rehabilitate the hospital, improve conditions by cleaning the hospital, and by providing supplies. I contacted businessmen.... The hospital was transformed completely and became one of the best hospitals in Somalia. News was passed to Mogadishu through the regional administration in Hargeisa about the work of those young professionals and the self-help scheme in the hospital. The news even reached the president's office. But they also heard that when these young people met, they talked about politics, so they were suspicious that there was a movement going on that was dangerous to the system and to the regime in Mogadishu.

Barre's government saw the self-help initiative as a potential threat. In August 1984, his government organised a trial of the youth in Hargeysa. One of Barre's appointees flew to Hargeysa to preside over the case. In a day, he concluded the hearing and issued a verdict.

The judge meted harsh sentences: death sentences to three fellows, thirty-year imprisonment sentences to ten men, and twenty-five-year sentences to seven. The remaining sentences ranged from three to eight years.

This trial was shabbier than the Rivonia Trial in 1963-1964, which was conducted by the Apartheid government in South Africa. There, Nelson Mandela received a life sentence for seeking an end to Apartheid rule. Dr Adan Yusuf Abokor was punished similarly for rehabilitating the Hargeysa Hospital in Somaliland. My schoolmate, Baaruud, received a death sentence for aiding Dr Adan and other like-minded youth.

Baaruud was one of the three condemned to death. Barre later converted his death sentence to life imprisonment. He served eight years of this sentence, all in solitary confinement.

I wanted to learn about a political prisoner's experience but remembered my resolution on managing deeply emotive topics, so I asked for a copy of his memoir, which I could not find for sale.

"It is out of print," Baaruud said calmly.

A day later, I received an electronic copy via email. I read it right away.

Baaruud's story was like no other memoir I had ever read. I knew the setting of the story and some of the protagonists. It vividly recounted the ordeal of the prisoners and the brutality of Barre's regime. The cruelty was surreal. Unimaginable. The conduct of the prisoners and their families was admirable and inspiring. The result is a portrait of a government at war with its people.

I wondered what it is like to lose youthful years. I took a copy of my résumé and deleted eight years of my thirty-year professional work experience to simulate a loss of productivity.

I wiped out years of investment in Universal Child Immunization and health sector reforms, two initiatives that benefited hundreds of thousands of children and women. The next casualty was disease control work in West Africa, notably against Guinea worm, yellow fever epidemics, vitamin A deficiency, and iodine deficiency disorders.

At that point in my simulation, the loss of productive years got to me, but I gritted my teeth and continued. I dropped references to humanitarian work from the résumé. This work involved aid to refugees from Ethiopia and Burundi and the victims of the 2004 Hindu-Kashmir earthquake in Pakistan.

The exercise was sobering. It gave me a clue to what Baaruud, a better man than I was at school, had lost in those eight years. Barre had robbed him of opportunities to serve his society and the world. The paper exercise was, of course, a poor simulation of the impact of confinement. It could not capture the psychological and emotional trauma of such brutal incarceration.

Baaruud did not seem bitter. He lived to serve Somaliland in other ways after the ousting of Barre's regime. In Maxamed Ibraahin Cigaal's cabinet, he served as the Minister for Rehabilitation, Resettlement and Reconstruction. Now he is fittingly the representative of Amnesty International in the country.

On another occasion in Hargeysa, I had supper with four other classmates from Sheekh Secondary School in the same week: Ismaciil, Cabdilaahi, Maxamed, and Diiriye. We were from the Sheekh Class of 1972.

Ismaciil landed an attractive civil service job and never left the country. Cabdillaahi and Maxamed went to the oil-rich Gulf States. They toiled in the desert heat for years and used their savings to cover higher education costs in America. Dr Diiriye, the reunion planner, split his time between Saudi Arabia and Somaliland.

The bond we'd developed in Sheekh Secondary School survived time and the Somali Republic's political upheavals. Nearly fifty years after our graduation from Sheekh, we still felt like brothers.

We discussed our travels and past reunions and shared information about other friends. We also recalled old jokes, including this one from Aw Maxamed, the generous canteen manager at our boarding school.

He used to say: "Waar quba shaaha. Mid kii hore ka wacan baa soo soc-da." *Folks, dump the tea you now have. A tastier brew is ready!*

We ended our banter just before midnight. We embraced again and promised to stay in touch. On the drive home with Dr Diiriye, I wondered if we should have prolonged our conversation at the reunion, but I banished the thought as soon as I remembered the smile on everyone's faces when we said goodbye. I thought we did well in bridging the decades of separation.

Mariam and I met on our veranda for our morning chat the next day. Noticing the grin on my face, she did not need me to confirm that the rendezvous with my high school friends had gone well. The endurance of friendships surprised both of us.

At that moment, I reflected on the career path of my high school friends in Hargeysa during my visit. Six were college graduates – one a physician, another an MBA, two engineers, and two PhDs.

The physician was the only recipient of a government scholarship. He did his first medical degree in Mogadishu and his post-graduate work in Turkey. Then he returned to Somalia where he worked unhappily for a few years. Afterwards, he left the country and stayed away until after the collapse of Barre's regime.

The rest of us used private methods to finance our education in the United States. After completing studies, everyone sought a career in places more hospitable than the Somali Republic under Barre.

The decision to stay away did not come lightly to any of us. From afar, we monitored Somalia's situation, particularly Barre's treatment of former schoolmates who showed readiness to assist in the country's development.

We were shocked when the government rounded up youth doing voluntary services. Stories like this dimmed the hope of educated youth returning to the Somali Republic while Barre was in control.

My quick reflection on human resources revealed Somalia's lost opportunities. This exercise barely scratches the surface of the massive brain drain. Somalia would have been far better off with a government harnessing the nation's resources. Barre's regime had become the proverbial Somali wolf that preyed on its offspring.

Departure

On 24 June, our visit to Somaliland ended. Mariam and I bid farewell to many relatives. Then we left Hargeysa for Nairobi the way we came.

The send-off at Hargeysa Airport was short to make the goodbyes easier for everyone. Once inside the building, we completed the airport formalities just as quickly and paused at the gift shop. We bought posters of Hargeysa, Borama, Taleex, Berbera, and the Sheekh Pass.

The Ethiopian flight was on schedule. We boarded the plane and roared down the runway designed for MiG fighter planes. Airborne, Mariam and I pressed hands. We had successfully finished our tour of the ancestral homeland without a hitch.

We sat near the front of the cabin, just behind business class. An old Somali woman slumbered on a bulkhead seat in front of us. She became restless and started gasping at take-off as the plane strained to gain altitude. Even the cabin crew sat quietly, their belts fastened.

A young woman sitting across the aisle, who I presumed to be a relative, noticed the distress signals. She ignored the cabin warning lights and promptly dealt with the older woman. The crisis ended in about five minutes, but the woman looked visibly exhausted. She took shallow breaths and clutched her seat arms.

I wondered how often this scene repeated yearly as the diaspora people shuttled between Somaliland and their new homelands. Cold and lonesome in Europe and North America, older people migrate south periodically. And because they have a higher rate of chronic illnesses, some require medical evacuation.

Elsewhere on the plane, other passengers stirred. When we landed at Bole, I noticed changes. A young White female who sat near us at the departure hall in Hargeysa discarded her hijab. One slender Black woman peeled off her abaya to reveal a loose pair of slacks and a sleeveless shirt. Another Black woman appeared in tight jeans and a low-cut sleeveless blouse which showed her cleavage.

We reached Nairobi safely after the stop at Bole. Steven, a freelance taxi operator we know, took us from the Kenyatta Airport through the hectic Nairobi traffic. In an hour, we were at our residence.

I returned from Somaliland with hundreds of pictures and stories of the civil war, reconstruction, and current affairs. My next task was processing this information. First, however, Mariam and I looked forward to a reunion with my nuclear family. All members were seldom in the same place at once.

My wife Laurie had relocated from Johannesburg to Nairobi a few months earlier to join the UNICEF Regional Office for East and Southern Africa. She was in Rwanda when Mariam and I returned from Somaliland, and my daughters were in transition between two worlds – school and work.

Sofia hosted us at our temporary residence in Nairobi. She prepared a home-cooked vegetarian meal, a welcome change from a diet that relied too much on meat. We had a rocket and feta salad, chickpea curry with brown rice or chapati, and cucumber and coriander yoghurt relish.

We swapped stories over dinner. My daughters shared ideas about Kenya and Somaliland where they have familial ties.

I sat across the table from my grown-up daughters. A cool breeze wafted intermittently, carrying drum and guitar notes of songs playing at a nearby building. This is a precious moment, I thought.

Yet, I was distracted. Returning from Somaliland, I wanted to discuss unfulfilled dreams, atrocities, and resilience, but I paused, asking myself questions. What is valuable advice to a young generation? What could I say about nationalism, tribalism, citizenship, and human rights?

Then I realised a speech was unsuitable for this audience, two graduates from Columbia and Yale. In addition, my daughters had heard me speak many times before. For nearly twenty years, they had watched my behaviour and listened to my stories about children and women in developing countries. They knew me. Clearly, I needed a new approach. At that instance, I felt relieved. My attention shifted to the chatter around me and the table of sumptuous food.

Identity

In Somaliland, people treated me as if I belonged there. They also extended the same courtesy to my daughter Mariam who was born in New York City but had never set foot in Somaliland.

In my birth country, Kenya, the picture was different, and it did not take long to be reminded that I was alien.

One day, I met a slender fellow in his late twenties at Westgate, Nairobi. He was an Uber driver. At the vehicle's arrival, the driver and I exchanged Uber-style greetings.

"Are you Jama?" he asked to ensure I was the right customer.

"Yes. Hello," I answered as I jumped into the back seat and shut the door.

"You are not a Kenyan!" he said instantly.

"How do you know that?"

"Your name. Jama isn't Kenyan," he replied, staring at the name on the digital screen.

"What is yours?"

"Paul."

"Ahaa. Paul is not a Kenyan name," I said in jest.

"It is."

"Paul is a biblical name," I asserted, no longer smiling. "And if this name makes you a Kenyan, I don't see why Jama, an African name, makes me a foreigner."

Paul frowned. I caught a glimpse of him in the rearview mirror. For the next few moments, we were silent. I welcomed the break in our conversation. I think Paul felt the same. His attention shifted to the road as his vehicle merged into traffic. Thankfully, Paul's driving was better than his argument.

The second incident occurred at the departure gate during a flight from Oliver Tambo International Airport, Johannesburg. The passenger sitting nearest to me was a woman in her thirties. She wore jeans and a sky-blue blouse. Her fingernails were polished and her hair relaxed. She balanced a laptop and a smartphone on her lap.

"Are you going to Nairobi?" she asked, looking up from the screen of her phone.

"Yes," I answered. "And you?"

"Nairobi. I'm a Kenyan."

"So am I," I replied, exuding pride in my recent status change after regaining Kenyan nationality. Thanks to the authors of the 2010 Kenya Constitution, I had regained citizenship.

Her partner, a young man of similar age, sat beside her, eavesdropping.

"But you don't look Kenyan!"

I took a deep breath before I spoke. "And what do Kenyans look like?"

She sat up, eyes no longer locked onto the cell phone.

"Your hair and your accent aren't Kenyan."

"But how does your identity test work in Kenya today, a country where we have people of African, Arab, Asian, and European descent?"

She had no ready answer. I watched her run her manicured fingers on the smartphone screen. Then I nudged her further.

"Have you been to the northeast part of Kenya?"

"Yes, I visited Isiolo."

"And what do people there look like?"

She became silent and played with her phone, not acknowledging the features of the people she met there. Incidentally, Isiolo is my birthplace and home to thousands of Somali and Borana people who look like me. Her partner noticed that and tried to help.

"We are all Africans," he said.

"This discussion is about Kenya," I cut him off.

The young man took the cue and retreated from the conversation.

"I think a hair test is a mark of ignorance," I said.

She mumbled and turned away to face her partner. A few minutes later, the airline announced that our flight was boarding.

The third episode occurred at a government office in Nairobi. I went there to apply for a national identity document (ID), the one document that every Kenyan needs to cross the street. Without it, a person cannot secure a SIM card, top up an M-PESA account (the digital money transfer application), open a bank account, or get a passport.

A friend accompanied me to the district office in Westlands, Nairobi, half a kilometre from my residence. I thanked him for the escort although I was sure I had all the required documents – my naturalisation paper, a recommendation from the Immigration Office, a copy of my birth certificate, a copy of my mother's birth certificate, a copy of my expired Kenyan passport, and passport photos.

I met a young officer who gave me forms to complete. Eagerly, I went to work until I tripped on a question of tribal affiliation. The effect was as jarring as a road bump in a speeding vehicle.

"Why does anyone need this information?" I spit out the thought whirling in my head. "Is this a colonial artefact?"

My first thought was to write "Kenyan" in every blank space, but I suppressed the urge.

Then I felt a friend's hand on my shoulder and heard his voice.

"Jama, just do it, then we will be out of here fast," he said.

I took a deep breath and then scribbled, "Somali, Isaak, Habar Yonis."

My next task was getting my fingerprints done. I stood in another line for half an hour and returned to the first officer with ink-stained hands.

"I did the fingerprints," I told the first officer, thinking he would tell me what would happen next.

"You have any brothers or sisters?" he asked.

"Yes," I replied, wondering what he would say next.

"Get a copy of your brother's or sister's ID."

"I must produce a sibling's ID to get my own!?"

Ostensibly, all the formal documents I presented were inadequate, so the question was: should I protest or compromise again?

I left the queue to call my eldest brother in Isiolo. He is hard of hearing and uncomfortable with smartphones. I shouted into the phone, ignoring the stern looks of those who glared at me because I failed to follow cell phone etiquette in public spaces.

My brother listened. "Haye," he said. *Yes.*

Before I hung up, I overheard my brother's instruction to a young relative with dextrous fingers. In minutes, I had the information I needed. Then I returned to the district officer, eager as a runner in a relay race to hand over the precious material. The young officer wasn't satisfied.

"Bring me a photocopy of the ID," he said.

I moved to another queue in front of a kiosk where my friend thought we could get help with the printing. He was right. I had two hard copies of my brother's ID a few minutes later. Then I re-joined my old queue, clutching photocopies of my brother's ID.

At this point, I had been at the district office for over two hours. I had museum fatigue, the kind that makes your bones ache but slightly worse because there was no place to sit. I envied fellow clients who were all younger than me, but there was no going back. I remained in the queue, hunched over.

As the line inched forward, I busied myself with removing the black stain I had picked up at the fingerprinting station. Finally, I stood at the finish line. The young officer looked up, collected the new document, and added it to my bulging file.

"Come back in a month," he said.

"Asante," I said, relieved to be done for the day.

A month later, I called the officer whose number I had obtained. "Do you have good news for me," I asked.

"No."

"What happened?"

"The application was rejected."

"What shall I do?"

"Go to Isiolo."

Isiolo is my birthplace, but I have not spent as much as a week there in the past forty-five years!

I wondered what went wrong. Did I miss a vital step of the process? Had I not left behind a file bulging with supporting documents and a letter from the Office of the President which I acquired after five years of vetting as part of the naturalisation process?

Instantly, I flashed back to 1972 when I applied for my first passport. It took me three months and numerous interventions to secure the document. I almost missed the start at my new school in Egypt.

Back then, Mr Wako Buneya, the member of Parliament from Isiolo, came to my rescue. He tolerated my frequent appearances at his residence, the only place I could find him. Buneya knocked at government doors until I had a passport.

I had celebrated prematurely, however. On close examination of the passport, I noted an error on the crisp document. It read "Trader" in bold letters as my profession. How did that happen? I wracked my brain and found one plausible answer for this mistake. Someone decided that I should be a trader like my father. I knew that title was on his passport in 1956.

How could I have introduced myself as a trader to the Egyptian Embassy and the university? I was close to tears.

A return to the Immigration Office meant more waiting and follow-up. Neither route was open to me. Mr Buneya had done enough for me. He also had many duties, including ministering to a stream of petitioners who regularly showed up at his residence.

So I gritted my teeth and prepared for an adventure in the land of the pyramids. In the fall of 1972, I probably became the only eighteen-year-old trader interested in medicine at Cairo University.

The clash between my passport and my real profession surfaced on the day that I went to the Immigration Office in Tahrir Square for a visa extension.

"Ya walad, anta taalib aw taajir?" said the unsmiling immigration officer. *Young fellow, are you a student or a trader?*

"Taalib, ya ustaad." *A student, sir.*

I had to bring a supporting document, so I went to the Kenyan Embassy in Cairo where I met the cultural attaché, a man with the memorable name Affande. It is Turkish for "Mister" or "Sir." Affande gave me a signed note. With it, I resolved the problem that the Nairobi official had created for me.

Fifty-plus years later, I needed the likes of Affande to clear obstacles to enjoy citizenship privileges fully – someone who knew that my brother's ID was an unnecessary requirement for my application, someone who could see that I had more proof of attachment to the country than most Kenyan citizens my age. I had a birth certificate from the colonial era, my mother's birth certificate, several expired Kenyan passports, and the ID that the Moi Government had issued to Somali-Kenyans after vetting my eligibility.

While lamenting my predicament, I came across an informative video, which Maxamed Adow, a Somali Kenyan and seasoned Al Jazeera correspondent, had prepared. The video, *Not Yet Kenyan*, shows Kenya's indifference towards Somali Kenyans.

Hopefully, the culture of marginalisation will end soon and the youth of Kenya will refrain from using wicked criteria like someone's hair texture to determine a person's citizenship.

Citizenship is not about acquiring administrative documents, but one cannot get by without them in Kenya. Without an ID card, a person cannot legally obtain a SYM card, seek employment, or vote. And without a passport, a student cannot pursue learning opportunities outside the country.

Despite these challenges, I have seen positive changes since Kenya and Somalia reconciled in 1967. Shortly after signing the peace agreement, my eldest sister returned home from exile in Kigoma, Tanzania, with three children. She dusted off my father's old home, one of the few Isiolo buildings with pinewood walls and a corrugated iron-sheet roof.

Twenty years later, my mother was back in Isiolo, a place she had left as a refugee at the height of the NFD crisis. She retraced the 2,000-kilometre route I took when I was six and in search of education. For my mother, fear for her grandchildren in northern Somalia was the motivation. Barre had unleashed security forces on Hargeysa. She took to the road at age eighty-five to protect her grandchildren. In 1991, another sister, fleeing the chaos in Mogadishu, landed in Isiolo with her children.

The draw for them was not the old home nor nostalgia about their wealth before the NFD crisis. It was security. Since then, Kenya's importance as a haven has only grown. Today, it is the favourite destination of Somali refugees and entrepreneurs. The latter group is investing substantially in various sectors of Kenya's economy.

I am hopeful that younger Kenyans will relate better and build an inclusive society in which someone's name does not set them apart.

PART II

The past has been a mint Of blood and sorrow
That must not be True of tomorrow.

Langston Hughes

Reflections

Mariam and I visited all the places on our itinerary and met many people. I started thinking of a return visit even before leaving Hargeysa. That said, the visit was not *entirely* smooth sailing.

I replayed scenes from the trip, including shaky conversations with relatives and friends who survived the civil war. Nothing in my schooling had prepared me for such encounters. I was uncomfortable, so I behaved like a student driver entering a freeway, cautious and edgy but eager to move forward. Fortunately, no one noticed my inner struggles.

The trip had one other effect. It forced me to challenge my younger self who believed honey was a by-product of independence. That child also thought people were of two kinds: those for and those against Somalia. I also believed that the Somali dream of unifying all Somali territories was achievable and that mighty nations deeply cared about weaker ones.

I would share a few things if I could speak to that child now. I would say that stewardship requires vision, discipline, and tolerance, that foreigners are not the only foes to fear, that self-interest motivates powerful nations, and that all Somalis need not be under one flag to thrive.

My reflections on the trip continued long after I had left Somaliland. I took notes and put them under separate headings as if preparing for the standard Somali prompt for the traveller: "*Bal warran.*" The phrase translates to, "Now report!" or "Give me the lowdown."

So here are my thoughts on the trip.

Achievements

Hargeysa is one of the safest cities I know. Its merchants managed cash in the open. Gold sellers worked from shelters without security. Women and children felt comfortable walking at night, and none of the elegant homes I visited employed security guards or had alarm systems.

Hargeysa was also safer than the capitals of all the countries sending soldiers to the Peacekeeping Force in Somalia. Somaliland set up its security alone; international peacekeeping would have been costly.

For example, I did a rough calculation of the costs of peace intervention in Somalia. Uganda is the longest-serving member of the United Nations Operation in Somali (UNOSOM). It has had 6,200 soldiers in the country since 2007. At a pay rate of $828 a month per soldier, the troops cost $60 million yearly or $720 million over the twelve years of work. Had peacekeeping ended, soldiers returning to Kampala would have boosted unemployment rolls in Uganda. The move would have left disgruntled ex-soldiers on the streets there.

Burundi earned $54 million annually from deploying its 5,400 soldiers. Undoubtedly, peacekeeping was an income-generating activity for the country. Pierre Nkurunziza protested when the African Union (AU) proposed scaling down the size of the deployment force in Somalia in 2018.

I saw other notable achievements. Somaliland established four credible presidential elections in twenty-eight years. The country used hybrid traditional and modern governing structures to achieve these results. This achievement sets Somaliland apart.

Over the same period, Somalia never had a single national election where people cast their votes. Uganda has had Yoweri Museveni as its president for the last thirty-three years, and Burundi was worse off. President Pierre Nkurunziza had established a dictatorship, cracking down on opposition. Many people left the country, following treacherous routes. Some acquired cholera along the way.

I remember the arrival of a boatload of refugees at Kigoma, Tanzania, in 2015. The WHO country director and I, the UNICEF country director, were at the port when the ship docked. It was a large iron vessel, a relic of the German occupation of Tanzania before World War I, but the boat was the only decent ship of its size on Lake Tanganyika. It helped the UN move the Burundian refugees from a cholera-stricken island to Kigoma and nearby camps.

At the docks, I saw the irony of Burundi's engagement in peacekeeping in Somalia and the exile of its citizens; however, I focused my attention on the humanitarian situation at hand.

There was progress in electrification in Somaliland. All the major towns and district capitals I visited had electric power. Even Oodweyne, a remote village where I attended primary school, had electricity.

New technologies were also spreading rapidly. Cell phone coverage was roughly seventy per cent of the country. This and other tools have spurred the use of moneyless transactions. I saw my first example of this system on my second day in Hargeysa.

"Jaamac, welcome to Hargeysa. Dr Diiriye booked this vehicle for you," said Mustafa, the owner of the rental car company. "Maxamed is your driver. Call me if you need any help. Safar wanaagsan." *Safe travel.*

Mustafa did not make me sign papers, pay a deposit, or give him a copy of my passport. The daily rate was USD 250, including fuel, the driver's fees, and unlimited mileage. I gasped when I heard the figure but accepted it. "Waa Hagaag," I said. *OK.*

At that moment, a skinny woman with a young boy approached us.

"Walaal icaawiya," she said. *Brother, help me.*

The request stumped me. I had no small US notes and no Somaliland currency. Mustafa came to my rescue.

"Walaal ninkani waa martiye iisheeg zaad lumber kaaga." *Sister, this man is a visitor. Tell me your Zaad account.*

"Eber, lix, sedex, todoba…" she read out the digits of her phone in Somali. "Haye, waa diyaar." *All done.*

Before leaving, she looked at him and asked how much he had sent. He told her. She blessed Mustafa and walked away.

My tally of achievements covers other fields. In aviation, people in Somaliland showed initiative and determination. Daallo Airlines set up vital links between Somaliland and the rest of the world. No other carrier offered services to a country emerging from civil war for nearly a decade.

In shipping, local entrepreneurs saved the day. They enticed freewheeling ships to dock at the Berbera Port, underwriting insurance that global giants refused to grant. Thus, the unrecognised country of Somaliland set up a maritime link with the outside world.

In education, rehabilitation of schools took place. There is phenomenal growth in tertiary institutions.

Today, Somaliland has hundreds of new and post-secondary schools. Local universities produce about 5,000 graduates every year. Under British and Barre's rule, Somaliland had only three secondary schools for boys, one intermediate school for girls, two vocational schools, and no universities.

One new school, Abaarso, is making waves. Jonathan Starr, an American philanthropist, founded it. The school helped more young people enter foreign universities in less than ten years than Britain had over seventy-five years of colonial rule. Abaarso has shown the impact of one generous and committed benefactor and the resolve of local students.

Today, Somaliland alone has five medical universities. Under General Barre, the Somali Republic had one.

Professor Saleebaan Axmed Guuleed singularly deserves credit for the advances in tertiary education. He established Amoud University, Somaliland's first institution of higher learning after the civil war.

"While Somalis are bickering and fighting among themselves, I want to educate thousands of students," he said in 1997. Professor Guuleed achieved this goal and paved the way for others to follow.

In the health sector, the work of two generous benefactors stands out. The first is Dr Edna Adan Ismail. Dr Edna, the daughter of a physician and the first Somali woman to train in the UK, is a stalwart figure in Somaliland. She is the founder and now director of the Edna Adan Maternity Hospital. This facility serves clients from all parts of a country where one in fifty women is at risk of dying from pregnancy-related causes. Dr Edna once served as the Minister of Foreign Affairs of Somaliland.

Dr Edna set up the maternity hospital in Hargeysa using her retirement funds as seed money for the project. Today, Edna Hospital is also the premier training centre for nurses.

Another Somali physician, Dr Maxamed Aaden Sheekh, founded a children's hospital in Hargeysa. Dr Maxamed, who is not from Somaliland, died before his dream had materialised. Still, his family members completed the work. They set up the new hospital in Hargeysa to reward the local community for promoting public safety after the civil war. Now, Dr Maxamed's gift serves thousands of children. His hospital is a testament to people whose generosity transcends regional and clan loyalty.

Hargeysa has also become the venue of the largest international book fair in East Africa, an event entering its twelfth year. The week-long event attracts writers, poets, publishers, and eager young readers. The initiative is the brainchild of Dr Jaamac Musse Jaamac, an academic. In 2019, delegates and dignitaries from twenty-three countries attended the opening ceremony. Few things show the can-do spirit of Somaliland better than this event that brings descendants of nomads together to celebrate books and printed works.

My note on achievements will be incomplete without mentioning the local elders and their role in peacebuilding and reconciliation. A notable example in this group is Xaaji Cabdikariim Xuseen Yuusuf, better known as Xaaji Cabdi Waraabe.

Xaaji Cabdi enjoyed a long life. His tenure stretched from the colonial era through military dictatorship and the first two and a half decades of Somaliland's second independence. Until his death in May 2019, Xaaji Cabdi was Somaliland's most experienced traditional leader, particularly in the upper house of Parliament known as the *Guurti*. He was also renowned for his wit and wisdom. He and others like him played a role generally reserved for international peacekeepers without receiving external sponsorship.

I discerned Xaaji Cabdi's commitment to peacemaking and his oratory skills from stories about his life. In one instance, he recounted how he became an orphan as an infant and grew up determined to avenge his father's death. When he reached maturity, he set off with three men, all armed. His destination was the homestead of the criminal's brother. Cabdi's relatives believed the brother's demise would cause more pain to the rival clan than the actual culprit.

On their approach to the homestead, Xaaji Cabdi and his companions received a warm welcome from the head of the household who had no clue about their actual mission. He slaughtered a ram to feed them and gave them a place to sleep.

When the time came to announce the purpose of the visit, Xaaji Cabdi concealed their goal.

"I am here to seek a bride from your family," he said. The host had no reason to doubt the statement because it was customary for young men to call on families with eligible daughters in that era.

A heavy rainstorm swept through the area a while later and shook the nomads' hut. On seeing this, the host promptly ran outside to fetch help. He brought materials to reinforce the dwelling and plug the leaks. As the visitors reposed, the host was thoroughly soaked and shivering.

Xaaji Cabdi was of two minds. He sought revenge but received kindness and hospitality. He turned to his companions and said, "A man with such compassion does not deserve a bullet. He is worthy of being someone's father-in-law."

After convincing his companions, Xaaji Cabdi talked with his host and disclosed the original plot and his reasons for revising the plan.

Kindness begot kindness. The astonished host agreed to give his daughter away in marriage to Xaaji Cabdi when she matured. The men parted amicably. In time, the couple wed and had fourteen children.

On another occasion, Xaaji Cabdi travelled to London with members of Parliament (MPs) from Somaliland. He followed the discussion between the Somali and British politicians through an interpreter.

"Does Somaliland have good relations with its neighbours?" one British MP asked. A Somali responded to the question, but moments later, Xaaji Cabdi asked for an opportunity to speak.

"Honourable members, you want to know about Somaliland's relationship with her neighbours. That is a fair question, but I want to remind you of what happened during World War II. Britain recruited our sons to fight its war. At that moment, we did not ask if your country had good relations with its neighbours.

"And now that Somaliland is seeking your help with attaining political recognition, is it fair that you ask about the relationship we have with our neighbours? And just so you know, we are good neighbours to everyone."

In writing down these achievements, I reminded myself not to forget a remarkable aspect of Somaliland's successes. The country has leapt forward with little international assistance.

There are, of course, challenges as well. Heading the list are clan politics, khat consumption, and environmental neglect. These I discuss next.

Clan Politics

Beneath Somaliland's remarkable stability runs an intricate substructure of clan relationships. People with blood ties live closer together, transact business together, and increasingly attend the same schools than they did before the civil war. This behaviour makes Hargeysa, the capital, an increasingly segregated city marked along clan lines.

Tribal politics run deep with threads everywhere – villages, towns, and throughout the diaspora. Many diaspora residents engage in tribal politics. They use the internet to promote their agendas and finance political candidates prioritising clan interests.

Fortunately, the clan virus has not turned virulent in Somaliland, thanks mainly to a wizened public and the influence of religious and traditional leaders. More than once, interclan tensions have surfaced, and some bloodshed occurred, but, ultimately, these eruptions cooled down, and sanity prevailed.

Should clan politics inflame emotions, it is very likely that Somaliland would lose the solidarity it forged through decades of struggles against General Barre's military dictatorship. It could become another failed state if this were the case.

To be sure, Somaliland cannot be complacent because the potential threat of clan politics is present and real. Clan affinity may even trump religiosity.

My fear of misreading the local situation vanished when I read the observation of a schoolmate from Sheekh with a deep knowledge of local affairs. "Loyalty to clans is stronger than loyalty to religion," he wrote in his memoir. This remark is a profound statement on Somaliland where Allah's exaltation appears on the flag and nearly every adult regularly goes to the mosque.

Another example occurred on my last days in Hargeysa when I visited Little Jigjiga, a neighbourhood on the western side of town, to visit a cousin. We agreed to meet after the sunset prayer. Returning from a visit to Las Geel, I rushed across town and reached the Gulaid Hotel just when the call to prayer came. The driver of our rented vehicle dropped me at the hotel and disappeared.

I slumped on one of the chairs at the teashop. Men rushed past me to the nearby mosque as the effects of the fluorescent light grew. I was the only errant Muslim during the period of devotion. A scene like this was uncommon in 1984. The teashops would have had more people sipping tea after the call to prayer. Hargeysa had changed. There are many new mosques and more significant settlements clustering along clan lines.

The scene prompted a question about faith and kinship. How does the believer reconcile his allegiance to tribalism with the tenets of his religion? The incongruence between piety and tribal loyalty is glaring.

Months later, I read about Islam and tribalism, the extreme form of kinship. The holy Quran said:

O you who believe, be persistently standing firm in justice as witnesses for Allah, even if it be against yourselves or parents and relatives.

O mankind! Indeed, We created you from a male and a female, and We made you nations and tribes that you may know one another. Indeed, (the) most noble of you near Allah (is the) most righteous of you.

In the Hadith, Wathila ibn Al-Asqa reported:

I said, "O Messenger of Allah, is it part of tribalism that a man loves his people?"

"No, rather it is tribalism that he supports his people in wrongdoing," the Prophet, Peace Be Upon Him, said.

"He is not one of us who calls to tribalism. He is not one of us who fights for the sake of tribalism. He is not one of us who dies following the way of tribalism," said Jubayr ibn Mut'ím, a narrator of Hadith.

Local clergy members provided a similar message in a 2019 interview that Cabdisalaan Hereri, a famous journalist from Somaliland, had conducted.

"Qabiilku meel xun buu marayaa," said Sheikh Joowhar, the renowned sheikh of Borama and a man who had offered counsel to Somaliland at critical stages for over three decades. "Habka manta waxaa ka nadiifsanaa habkii hore," he added. *People conducted themselves better in the old than they do today.*

"Tribalism is one of the sicknesses of the Somali people wherever they are," added Sheekh Cali Gadhle. "It is the impediment to progress, self-reliance, and standing of Somalis among nations."

Hereri also collected testimonies from members of communities suffering from ethnic strife.

"How did the problem affect the area?" the journalist asked the locals.

"All social services stopped," replied the mayor of the town. "A water project we expected to start four years ago was suspended. The health centre and sixteen local schools closed."

District officials from the two feuding clans said they could not be in the same place for months because of the heightened hostilities.

"Based on your experience, what message do you have for communities where there may be some tensions?" Hereri asked.

"Dhibaatada waxaa garanaya ninkey imika hayso . . . Waanu uga digeeynaa. Alana waxaanu ugabaryeeynaa inaanu gaadhsiinba . . . Waxa dhacay waad aragtaan: hobol la'aanta, dibudhaca, habsaanka, iyo dadkii ehelka ama labadii inaabtiga iyo isuahaa walaalo inaaney isu gudbin ama isarkikarin. Coolaadi taasey leedahay," said the deputy mayor. *The one facing a problem knows best. Let [our experience] serve as a warning. We pray to Allah that [others] don't reach this point. You can see what happened: bereavement, backwardness, delays, and the loss of social contact among people with blood ties, including cousins and blood relatives.*

Somali poets have debated tribalism. Some urged their kinsmen to wage war. Others entreated their relatives to seek peace and good neighbourliness.

And yet, there are staunch critics of the system.

Cabdillaahi Suldaan Timacade is the most ardent critic. He earned a special tribute from Northerners for serenading Somaliland's attainment of independence on 26 June 1960. Yet, Timacade is better known for his uncompromising commentary on tribalism and earned an exalted position among Somalis for his warnings about the social impact of tribalism. Contemporary poets use him as a reference for their lyrics on this subject.

In one poem, Timacade cited tribalism as a Somali curse. According to him, Somalis who create obstacles for each other's advancement do not hear consul.

> Duba madaxa wa iskala dhacnaa daaín ebikeede
> Dul iyoo hoosba waan ugu dhigay waa dix dhagaxeede
> Wixi hore usoo daashaday bey degashanaysaaye

> *A hammer is the Somali tool for knocking each other down*
> *No one pays attention to counsel softly or loudly stated*
> *And they embrace that which [tribalism] holds them back.*

> Doc haday u wada jeedsatooy dhowrto danaheeda
> Oo duul walaala ah tahay ooy duunka ka heshiiso
> Dadka kama yaraateene ways dabar jaraysaaye.

In the second line of the verse, Timacade imagines Somalis without the handicap of tribalism. In brotherhood and agreement, Somalis can compete favourably with other societies. Then his optimism fades quickly because Somalis tend to undercut each other.

Timacade's observations hold today for Somalis in various parts of the world.

Maxamed Xaashi Dhamac Gaariye, a schoolmate at Sheekh, was another prominent poet who addressed tribalism. He was a moderating factor during the heady days following the ousting of Barre's army. There were too many men with guns. The movement, which had concentrated on military action to dislodge Barre's forces, was slow in developing a strategy to govern the liberated territory, so clan-based violence erupted periodically. Gaariye could not bear the continued suffering of Northerners and the rivalry among different interest groups.

Addressing a peace conference in Burco in the mid-1990s, Gaariye talked about the short-sightedness of various factions (tribal groups) jostling for cabinet seats and senior appointments. He pointed out that there were not enough top jobs to go around.

"Promote justice, a commodity you can share with many people," he said.

Gaariye was right. Cabinet seats and civil service posts are limited, and allocating these posts is a zero-sum game. Justice is different. It is an infinite construct.

The theme of justice is the main message from another renowned citizen of Somaliland, Xasan Ciise Jaamac. Jaamac, a fellow schoolmate at Sheekh and my dormitory leader, won one of the coveted scholarships to Britain. He studied law but left a promising career to become a founding member of the movement, which waged the struggle against Barre's regime. After Barre's ousting, he became the first deputy president of the country. When Axmed Xasan Cawke, a veteran journalist from Somaliland, asked what his wishes were for the people of Somaliland, Jaamac stressed justice.

Tribalism has another problem. It confuses children who are the product of interclan marriages. The induction to tribalism starts very early in life. This custom confuses children.

I first fully grasped this dilemma in children in the mid-1990s. A bright seven-year-old child, the son of a Somali colleague from Tanzania, heard a story he could not understand, so he approached his father.

After hearing stories of ethnic clashes in Somaliland, the boy asked in Kiswahili, "Aabo, ni kweli hoyo na aabo wana pigana?" *Father, are my mother's and father's people truly fighting?*

The story baffled the child and left the father speechless.

"How could I explain the crazy system, Jama?" the father asked me at a dinner in his house in Dar es Salaam.

The kinship web has long tentacles. It caught up with me unexpectedly in Burco. Guuleed knocked on my door about an hour after we checked into a hotel.

"Odeyaal baa halkan jooga," he said. "Geeri ayey Burco uyimaadeen." *There are elders here dealing with the ramifications of a recent death.*

The deceased had been a policeman. He died while on duty near Burco. The authorities followed a two-pronged strategy to administer justice. They arrested the perpetrator of the crime but invited local elders to intervene. The actions helped reconcile the communities on the most appropriate punishment. Had they not done so, it was conceivable that a hot-headed relative would take revenge, thus escalating the hostilities.

I was a tourist and didn't expect to be part of a public debate on a criminal case, but our brief stay in Burco changed that. The elders from Go'da Weyn, who coincidentally were lodging in the same hotel, requested an audience as soon as they learnt of our presence.

My brother Max and I met everyone's definition of an elder. We had kinship ties to the community of Go'da Weyn and seniority in age and education, which most people now consider an asset.

Although Max and I appreciated the honour of being referred to as elders, we pleaded with Guuleed to excuse us from the deliberations. I felt like a candidate for jury duty, fishing for reasons to escape.

We tried but could not wriggle our way out of this situation, so we agreed to a brief meeting with Xariir, the head of the delegation from Go'da Weyn. He shook my hand and told me we had met more than fifty years earlier in Oodweyne.

"You were a student. I was a young camel boy," he said.

He wore a chequered macawis (sarong), a short-sleeved shirt, a gold-embroidered hat, a shawl, and sandals. Holding a walking stick with silver decorations in his right hand, he sat up straight and spoke in a calm, deep voice that made us focus.

Our meeting lasted half an hour. We listened to Xariir and commended his role in the reconciliation efforts. Then we expressed regret that we could not change our tight travel plans, but we set a time and place for another rendezvous with him.

On our behalf, Guuleed donated money to help the families of the deceased. They were incurring costs while staying in Burco until the deliberations ended. Government officials and community leaders worked together to resolve the matter.

The incident made me wonder how the kinship system in the Somali Republic under General Barre had become a virulent strain, creating a failed state. Is poverty a cause of instability? I settled on leadership as the critical factor, drawing on other African examples.

I saw extreme poverty, poor education, and physical isolation in parts of Tanzania, yet Tanzania's treatment of each of its communities impressed me. President Julius Nyerere ruled a country with 120 tribes. Nevertheless, Tanzania maintained civility and security while Somalia was tearing itself apart. People with different languages and religions live together in Tanzania amicably.

After retiring from the United Nations, my friend Ahmed Magan and I visited Rwanda. We found it safe, vibrant, and a model of hygiene and cleanliness for all of Africa. After ending the genocide, President Paul Kagame harnessed his fractured society's energy to build a stronger nation.

With all their swagger, Somalis have not matched the performance of the soft-spoken Tanzanians, nor have they drawn inspiration from the grit of the Rwandans who brought their country back from the brink and made it a model of cleanliness.

Khat

Somaliland is wrestling with two invasive plants: garanwaa and khat. Garanwaa, a shrub of South American origin, is ubiquitous. I saw groves of garanwaa on the riverbanks of Oodweyne, the outskirts of Burco, and in empty plots in Hargeysa, but no one could tell me how it reached the country.

Khat followed trade routes. Today, it is readily available in every region of Somaliland.

"What does the number over there mean?" Mariam asked one day, pointing to a wooden stall in front of a shop in Dumbuluq, Hargeysa. The colourful booth had a number inscribed on it.

"That is a place to buy khat," Saamiya said. "The number identifies the supplier. Hargeysa has thousands of stalls like this."

Thus, we began discussing the plant's implications on health, the economy, and the environment.

Khat is a mildly narcotic plant grown in Ethiopia, Kenya, and Yemen and is traded legally in these countries. Its botanical name is *Catha edulis*. Ask a user and he will gladly tell you about its virtues. It gives the consumer a buzz, excitement, and a good feeling. The Somali word *marqaan* sums it all up. It refers to the euphoric feeling derived from khat.

Much of the khat comes from eastern Ethiopia where Somaliland has long enjoyed social and commercial ties. Kenya and Southern Yemen also produce khat. However, these countries do not have supply networks with Somaliland.

Coffee, another Ethiopian product that helps users stay alert, has not won over Somalis. It is cheaper than khat and has a longer shelf life. Yet coffee consumption remains low while khat consumption is strikingly high.

Cathinone, the main ingredient of khat, degrades soon after harvest. Traders, therefore, are ever in a hurry to deliver a fresh product to eager customers.

I have not seen written accounts of the history of khat in Somaliland. One oral history asserts that pious men used the plant to stay awake during long meditation hours. The habit spread to truck drivers, musicians, and urbanites.

My earliest memory of khat stems from the 1960s. I was in Hargeysa, then the northern capital city and home to a growing number of civil servants. Urban population growth after independence boosted the khat trade. Residents of urban centres, particularly men, had disposable income and free time. I don't remember seeing khat in Isiolo in 1960 although my hometown was only about fifty kilometres from the khat heartland of Kenya.

Over time, khat made inroads into Somali communities, impacting white-collar workers and secondary school boys in urban centres. People in rural areas seldom used khat. Women held out for a long time. But in the mid-1960s, stories began circulating about khat parties, at which both men and women indulged. Such parties took place mainly in the red-light districts in towns.

Consumption peaked on weekends, holidays, and after payday each month. On those occasions, civil servants stayed up at night using khat and slept late the following day.

I've used khat about two dozen times – in Somalia and Kenya and once in Minneapolis.

In the late 1980s, I was a graduate student at the University of Minnesota and the only person with Somali roots in the Twin Cities. One day, an American friend asked if I could spend time with three new Somali arrivals. They were refugees from Ethiopia. I readily agreed.

The fellows were adjusting well to the harsh Minnesota winters. Occasionally, I saw signs of homesickness in them. One of the fellows enrolled at the University of Minnesota. He is now a successful banker. Once, I invited the fellows to a khat party to remember Jigjiga and Dire Dewa, their hometowns, where khat parties were popular. I got the khat from a Yemeni supplier in New York City. The merchant used express mail to send the product to Minneapolis. Khat was not illegal in the United States at that time.

I took pictures of the khat, the mail-order packaging, the venue, and my friends before and after the khat party. Although we traded nostalgic stories, the party was not worth all the effort I invested in it.

In Kenya and Somalia, I knew many regular khat users. Some were relatives; others were friends. Although everyone discouraged young people from using khat, some of those giving us advice indulged in the habit. They sent a child to the local shops if they needed cigarettes or Coca-Cola for their khat parties. My guardian disapproved of the habit, and despite lapses, I followed his advice.

I remember the first khat party I attended in Hargeysa. Following my experienced friends' lead, I removed my shoes, replaced my trousers with a colourful macawis, and reclined on a mattress with covers and pillows.

I recall a room with windows shut and curtains drawn. In one corner lay a small charcoal burner spewing incense. The sweet scent mingled with the cigarette fumes circulating in the airless room.

Like a formal dinner, everything had a proper place. The khat wrapped in a napkin was one arm's length to my right, the soft drinks in the middle islands, and shoes near the entrance. I watched an experienced friend take the first steps: stroke a branch of khat, break off the tender shoot, and put it in his mouth.

I followed his example. At the first bite of khat, I winced. I took sips of tea and Coca-Cola to cut the bitterness. The drinks injected an added caffeine dose into my body. I also took sips of water to clear the perpetual dryness in my mouth.

The group conversation soon dissolved into several bilateral chats. Somali music spewed continuously from a tape player. At 5:30 pm, as if by conditioning, everyone tuned to the news on the BBC Somali broadcast.

Our chatter resumed after the news bulletin. Four hours later, the khat party was over. Then we took turns in the bathroom to freshen up, put on our street clothes, and dispersed.

The buzz from the khat faded in an hour or two. After that, I developed an awkward twitch of the lips from an afternoon of chewing khat. The next day, the twitching ended, but I developed sores in my mouth. These cuts, too, healed naturally in two days.

On another occasion, I joined a party with Maxamed Moogeh, the most popular male Somali singer in my school days. The setting was similar, but the company of Moogeh, the soft-spoken teacher with a golden voice, was a treat. His rendition of "Raaxeeye," a classic Somali song, and anti-regime songs ("Dadka ha iska weyneyn" and "Aduunyooy") was worth all the second-hand smoke I inhaled at this khat party.

Between 2013 and 2017, the average annual import of khat into Somaliland was 34 million kilograms, according to the Somaliland Statistical Department. At USD 20 a kilogram, the price tag for this recreational commodity was $680 million a year. This estimate is conservative. A retail merchant sells khat in fractions of a kilogram. A quarter of a kilogram of khat, which people call *mijin*, fetches $3 to $12. High-grade khat costs more than that.

Somaliland's annual expenditure on khat was forty-seven times the nation's budget for education, ninety-one times that for health, and 378 times the investment in water in 2019.

The drug's financial drain came into focus when I examined the expenditure on khat over time. The spending was USD 255 million in four and a half months. This amount was sufficient to finance the vital Berbera-Wajaale road. In seven months, the money spent on khat could have covered the expansion of the Berbera Port, Somaliland's most ambitious infrastructure project.

Undoubtedly, though, khat generates livelihood for many and revenue for the customs department.

In short, the expenditure on khat buys hallucinations, euphoria, and unhealthy lifestyles. Khat also dramatically contributes to the proliferation of plastic waste.

Until recently, khat relied on banana leaves as wrapping. When discarded, the leaves became fodder for urban goats. The rest of the material decomposed. The situation has changed. Nowadays, khat merchants wrap bundles of khat in plastic for sale at retail stalls.

The tally of plastic sheets used to wrap khat tops the two million mark in a single month. The figure is higher if you assume that each of the 2.8 million kilograms of khat sold monthly gets a separate wrapper. This plastic takes over two hundred years to break down.

Stopping there overlooks another associated environmental risk. The khat trade boosts the sale of soft drinks and bottled water in Somaliland. These products, in turn, contribute to environmental pollution and a higher intake of sugary drinks.

If only one-third of adult males use khat regularly and only ten per cent of this group drink a bottle of water daily, they will discard 30,850 bottles daily.

Over fifteen days of khat use in a month, the tally of empty bottles will be close to half a million. There will be around six million empty plastic bottles from khat use alone yearly.

End to end, the discarded bottles in a year make a rope ninety-four kilometres long, almost equivalent to the distance between Hargeysa and Borama. The picture may be worse because I have not added the plastic bottles that non-khat users dump into the environment.

The lack of a public water system in urban centres is also a culprit in the proliferation of plastic waste in Somaliland. It increases people's dependence on bottled water, which further causes environmental damage. As the saying goes, however, a loss for one may be a profit for another. Bottled water companies will continue to rake in money if the public lacks access to potable water.

There are more than a dozen such bottled water companies in Somaliland. Similar investments in public water supply systems are sorely lacking. Instead, investments go towards temporary measures. Hargeysa now has a massive fleet of private water truckers. The trucks fill a gap in service delivery, but they are a nuisance on the major roads and contribute to traffic accidents.

With so much plastic, it's no wonder I saw evidence of dumping in scenic areas like the Sheekh Pass. On our trip from Burco to Berbera, we stopped briefly at a viewpoint on the Sheekh Pass to take pictures. The distant landscape was breathtaking. But there were discarded plastic water bottles and other rubbish at our feet, and there were no trash cans.

Las Geel, another historic site in Somaliland with ancient cave paintings of cattle, dogs, and the ancestors of Somalilanders would have suffered the same fate had it not been for staff guarding the place. The day we visited the site, the men asked us to leave our water bottles near the exhibit hall before walking us up a hill to view the ancient paintings. As we were preparing to leave, they burnt the trash.

Gacan Libaax Mountain is not safe either. I saw evidence of dumping there although the number of visitors is still small because of bad roads. The site needs protection before the traffic increases and the environmental damage becomes irreversible.

Plastic waste is a global problem, and Somaliland is no exception. I recall Kenya's experience. Khat is legal merchandise, but the government introduced measures to curtail the circulation of plastic. Kenya's ban on the sale of single-use plastic bags went into effect in 2017.

The impact of the policy is already noticeable. City streets are appreciably cleaner. A few years ago, the picture was different. Thorn trees, which trapped loose plastic, looked like scarecrows. In drought conditions, livestock ate cardboard and plastics.

I remember a desperate situation from my visit to Garissa in 2005. A severe drought affected the district. I saw many dead sheep and goats. Loose plastic stuck out of the rib cages of carcasses. Undoubtedly, the lack of rain triggered a crisis, but the plastic must have hastened the animals' demise.

Improving public water supply systems is one answer to the proliferation of plastic waste, and banning the sale of khat is another. As we know, khat sales in Somaliland and plastic circulation go hand in hand. The trade of khat boosts the circulation of plastic wrappers with long-lasting environmental effects.

Somaliland could draw lessons from the UK, which banned the sale of khat in 2012. The initiative created an intense public debate. Some people, including government officials, supported the ban. Others vehemently opposed it.

The debate focused on the social and economic impacts. Advocates of the ban cited the health and social consequences of using khat. Opponents emphasised the plan's financial benefits. They pointed out that non-drinkers of alcohol use khat as a pastime.

Five years later, I read comments from Somali advocates of the khat ban in the United Kingdom. They argued that Somali immigrants' prospects of social integration into British society were better because Somalis were no longer "distracted" by khat. Men were also spending more time with their families.

Somaliland has not yet embraced a similar debate. When it does, I think the contest will mirror the United Kingdom's. But advocates of khat use are likely to prevail by the strength of numbers alone. They may also exaggerate khat's economic value, overstate the plant's use for recreational purposes, or downplay its health and social impacts.

Still, Somaliland can no longer ignore the effects of khat. New knowledge about the plant has become available in the past decade. The World Health Organisation (WHO) and the US National Institute of Health (NIH) have warned about its use. Under the "long-term effect," the NIH cited heart attacks and abdominal problems such as ulcers and stomach inflammation. Under psychotic reactions, NIH named fear, anxiety, grandiose delusions, hallucinations, and paranoia.

The strategy for banning khat in the United Kingdom may not work in Somaliland. In the former, the initiative came from the government, and the general population was suspicious of the Somali habit. In Somaliland, non-users are fewer in number than in Britain. They include women and children who do not control the levers of power.

Despite the odds, the country needs a long-term policy on the khat trade, and advocates for a ban will require all the support they can get.

Khat has inspired commentary from poets, who can play a vital role in any campaign to win hearts and minds against this drug.

Cilmi Siciid Jaamac, composed the following verses addressing khat use. Waa geedka qaybaha bulshadu qaran ku waayeen ee

Waa geedka kala qaybiyaye qaarba meel digayee
Waa geed qaloociyo xumaha lagu qorsheeyaaye
Waa geed qaraar oo hadana lagu qamaamayee
Qori iyo garaabadii dhacdaa qariyay dowgiiyee
Waxaa laamiyadii sii qaribey qolofti geed kaase
Qashin buu ka dhigey suuqyadhii quruxda weynaa ee
Niman uu qaribay qaadku oo quus ah baa jira ee
Qaarna wuuba qaatay oo wax kale kuma qadeeyaanee
Qabsin iyo xanuun aan lagaran buu kuridey qaaree.

Translation:
Khat distracts communities from nation-building
Khat creates barriers that keep groups apart
Khat creates opportunities for conspirators
Khat is a bitter leaf with a powerful attraction
Khat is the ruin of our beautiful streets
It is khat leftover that has clogged our ways
Khat has spoiled men [rendered them impotent] and left others desperate
Turning others into addicts with no other desires,
Suffering from constipation or other diseases.

Environment

Somaliland is renowned for its sparse vegetation, water scarcity, and short season of splendour after the monsoon rains. The plateaux region receives 300 to 600 millimetres of rainfall in a typical year. This territory covers much of the central and western parts of the country. Hargeysa's annual rainfall is 440 millimetres. Burco receives roughly half that amount.

People's livelihoods have depended on livestock for centuries. The oldest proof of this relationship appears at Las Geel, a cave with ancient paintings. Farming took place in the few wetter zones in the country, mainly the areas southwest of Hargeysa.

The ecosystem of the region has markedly changed in recent times. The vegetation cover is thinner, and the drought frequency is higher than it used to be. Cattle and horses, two of the country's primary resources 130 years ago, have almost vanished.

Several factors are to blame for the environmental problems. Some are political, others cultural or natural.

One political event with far-reaching environmental consequences occurred in 1954. Britain, the colonial ruler of Somaliland at the time, ceded the winter grazing land of Somali nomads (better known as the Haud) to

Ethiopia. Britain cited the Anglo-Ethiopian Treaty of 1897 to justify its decision although Somalis had no part in the Ethiopian-British talks on territories. The nomads limited their southern movement to avoid harassment from Ethiopian authorities. Harassment meant taxes, confiscation of livestock, and, in extreme cases, destruction of wells to teach the Somali nomads a lesson. I heard such stories when I was young.

These actions, in turn, forced livestock to stay longer in shrunken territory, which led to overgrazing.

In the late 1950s, Britain excavated earth dams in the livestock grazing areas. Margaret Laurence, the wife of the project engineer, covered the initiative in her memoir, *The Prophet's Camel Bell*.

The dams provided some relief and then pain. The water attracted livestock, and the higher the livestock traffic, the faster the pace of desertification of the land around the dams. Regrettably, the dams silted, and some virtually disappeared a few decades after the British returned to their isles.

Nomads themselves have played a vital role in the environmental crisis. Their contribution is most evident in the way they treated the local vegetation. The error is palpable in a joke that Somalis tell about themselves. The self-deprecating joke goes like this: Somalis have embraced only one innovation, and with it, they have wreaked havoc on the environment.

The item is a *gudimo*, a primitive axe forged from scrap metal. The tool is ubiquitous in the countryside where a nomadic family moved camp twice or thrice a year. Each time a family moved, they cut down acacia branches to make animal enclosures. Millions of gudimo cuts have left indelible marks on a fragile ecosystem over centuries.

As the name implies, Oodweyne, meaning "Big Bush," once had dense vegetation. In 2019, I found the ground cover thinner than in 1963, and the once-rich wildlife in the surrounding country has vanished.

Hadraawi, the greatest living poet in the Somali language, had this to say in about a place near Burco called Libaaxley, "The Lion Territory": "Libaaxley is barren today. A hare cannot find a place to hide."

I discovered something similar. Driving from Hargeysa to my brother's farm one morning, we crossed the Golis Plateau. The land stretched under a blue sky for kilometres. I saw herds of Somali sheep, famous for their black heads, white coats, and fat tails. As I gazed at the rural scene, I rolled down the car window to get the full effect of the breeze. My fellow passengers were unmoved until they sighted a solitary Thomson's gazelle.

"Look! Look!" everyone shouted. I scanned the horizon and saw a gazelle galloping away. At a safe distance, she paused and looked back at us nervously, twitching her short tail.

On that day, I grasped the depth of the environmental change in this area over several generations. British wildlife hunters who visited Somaliland left detailed accounts of a landscape teeming with antelopes and other wildlife. Several expeditions landed in Berbera, hired camel caravans, and headed south for big game hunting. At the Golis Plateau, they found agreeable weather and large herds of wild animals, including lions, rhinos, leopards, and antelopes of many kinds. The lone antelope probably came from that stock. The climate is still pleasant, but much of the wildlife has disappeared, and the vegetation is thinner.

Charcoal burning caused considerable damage to the environment as well. The trade flourished shortly after the civil war when people struggled to survive. Many giant acacias vanished, leaving behind the young trees. A local elder who hiked with me in this area said, "Waa la gubey dhirtii waaweyneyd. Dhuxul ayaa laga dhigey." *Someone turned the trees into charcoal.*

The man pointed out shallow ditches dotting the red soil. Chips of charcoal covered the perimeter of each pit. "These are the tell-tale signs of the tree-burning operations," he said. "The chips are indestructible. They linger for decades."

People spoke of weak regulatory bodies and how this weakness has spawned unacceptable practices, including tree cutting, land grabs, and inattention to matters of common interest, including the environment.

Public assets had become a new frontier of conquest in the country after the eviction of forces loyal to General Barre. Fences and concrete walls popped up everywhere. A multi-storey building squats on the old Hargeysa soccer field. Nearby, Reece Elementary School looks beleaguered behind a stone wall like an old tortoise. Truckers have turned the children's playground into an outdoor vehicle repair shop cluttered with garbage and grease.

Axmed Gurey, Hargeysa's best intermediate school, has lost playgrounds. Private settlements have encroached into its boundaries, and victims of a recent drought pitched makeshift shelters in the school compound. Government villas in Shacabka, the district reserved for colonial officials before Somaliland gained independence, had a similar fate. Most of the buildings have become personal property. Hargeysa also lost the Women's Club, the only institution that once offered women vocational training.

Berta Xoriyada, the Independence Park in the heart of Hargeysa, exists only in name. One section of this park is a barren octagon. Another corner is a small nursery, and a third now has a cluster of government buildings. The challenges for the small environmental ministry in an unrecognised state are daunting: deforestation, indiscriminate rubbish dumping, endangerment of water sources, and over-harvesting of frankincense-producing trees. Overseas traders of frankincense alone can torpedo the work of researchers aiding local protection of trees that deserve World Heritage designation.

Hargeysa sorely lacks playgrounds for children and public spaces for recreation. Increasingly, the settlement pattern is segregated along clan lines. The Owls, a fictitious name, cluster in one place, the Hawks in another. The Eagles and Roosters are in the third corner of the town. Mention a neighbourhood, and someone can identify the clan affinity of those who reside there.

"Where are you going?" asked a taxi driver I hired one day from the Old Indian Line neighbourhood. It was about 2 pm.

"Guri Masalaha kuyaal, iyo Ambassador Hotel," I said. "Waxaan doonayaa inaan soo qaato computer-keeygii. Dabadeed, qado iyo internet udoonto hudheelka Ambaasador." *A house at Masalaha and the Ambassador Hotel. I want to pick up my computer from the house, then go to the hotel for lunch and internet access.*

"Anba maan qadeeynin," he said. *I haven't eaten lunch myself.*

"Maxaa dhacay?" *What happened?*

"Quudkii caruurta ayaan maantoo dhan ku mashquulsanaa." *I have been working hard for my children's daily bread.*

He took a long pause and then hurled another question at me. "Ma Garxajis baad tahay?" *Are you from the Garhajis clan?*

This line of inquiry is bizarre, I thought. I did not see a relationship between a taxi ride and clan identity.

Another day, I decided to see more of the local environment and drove to Naasa Hablood to escape the congestion and take sunset pictures of the famous Hargeysa landmark. The driver of the Land Cruiser and I approached the hills from the south. A foul smell greeted us near Naasa Hablood. It came from the waste dumps of Hargeysa's slaughterhouses. Soon, however, we cleared the stench. North of the Hargeysa Bypass, I found scenery that made the excursion worthwhile. Ahead of us lay a pristine landscape with a cool, refreshing breeze. The topography was variable, and the indigenous vegetation (mostly acacia) was bountiful.

The conical hills dominated the view to the west, a small tog in the north, a ridge in the east, and the Hargeysa Bypass in the south. At dusk, golden sun flares hung behind the hills like a curtain, and Hargeysa lights glittered in the south and southwest. Suddenly, there were the outlines of a grand park for a city that had lost most of its public spaces. Fortunately, access to this site will vastly improve when the Hargeysa Bypass is completed.

The 840-acre park that Frederick Law Olmstead and Calvert Vaux designed nearly 150 years ago in New York City is one of the most famous recreation sites in the world today. At inception, Central Park provided an escape for thousands of New Yorkers huddled in poor, filthy, crowded neighbourhoods. Now it is one of the city's great attractions, a retreat for millions of visitors, and a breathing space for a town with thousands of vehicles. Visitors' income and ethnicity do not matter at all there.

Hargeysa's current and future populations deserve an escape from crowded and littered spaces as is possible with Central Park. Maybe this is the spot, but this potential may be forever lost if the encroachment and waste dumping rates continue.

• • •

Somaliland lacks surface water. Rainwater comes in spurts and then flushes through a network of togs to low-lying areas – the Somaliland coast and the territories to the south and southeast.

Pain from thirst is palpable in the Somali language. People have as many descriptors for water scarcity as the Inuit do for snow.

For thirst alone, Somalis have many words. The most common ones are *oon*, *surmi*, and *haraad*, but there are additional terms covering extreme conditions, such as thirst-related incoherence, or desperate measures involving the saving of lives during drought.

Nearly eight decades of British control of Somaliland and sixty years of self-governance have not quenched this thirsty nation, and recent trends are worrisome.

In Hargeysa, the tog, once the primary source of water for the city and one of its prominent landmarks, is dying. There is little acacia lining its banks – no wild fruit-bearing gob trees. Sand, the most generous gift of a tog, has vanished.

I also saw mounds of ubiquitous trash, including household garbage, plastic, waste from garages and restaurants, and construction debris such as marble chips, concrete, and rusty iron sheets at every crossing. The trash pile grew daily as if the river competed with the city's growth.

Togs have received little attention although they shaped the settlement and migration patterns of the inhabitants. Without togs, Hargeysa, Burco, Oodweyne, Ber, Mandheera, Lafaruug, Dacarbudug, Xaaxi, and Cadaadley would be non-existent. Without the bounty of togs, the Nugaal Valley could not have sustained herders, horsemen, and two decades of rebellion against British rule.

There is another remarkable thing about togs that seldom gets attention. A tog is attractive for picnics and hikes in the dry season. The sand offers an excellent surface for sporting activities, especially volleyball.

The water problem is too big for Somaliland. It is a developing country with few resources and limited technical skills, thereby limiting its ability to harvest sufficient rainwater annually. International recognition will undoubtedly open doors for improved cooperation in many fields, including water conservation, but Somaliland cannot delay action until it has secured recognition.

The country urgently needs a bold initiative to set a thirsty land on a sustainable path. An essential first step is the declaration of water as a strategic resource. It is a cause that calls for national sacrifice and more significant investments, starting with the money now spent on khat! Another measure is the protection of waterways, the national arteries for water circulation. A third is harnessing the resolve that helped the nation achieve peace and security in a volatile region and tackling environmental challenges.

Politicians, religious leaders, traditional elders, and educators have a primary role in this endeavour. Schools and tertiary institutions must teach, research, and promote conservation and innovation.

Amnesia

In Borama, a relative talked to me about her memorabilia.

"Jaamac, I have the photos you took," she said, grinning during our first reunion over four decades.

My flashback was instant. She was referring to a photo shoot we did at an orange orchid in Borama in 1969. The handsome subjects were my older brother's fiancé and her sister.

The photos were a time capsule. They outlasted the Republic of Somalia, which sent my brother, an officer in the special commando forces, to the Borama area, where he met his future bride. Peace and happiness were in the air at the time. Somalia was not at war with itself, and the chronic tensions between Ethiopia and Somalia were low.

My relative had quickly recovered the photos because Borama escaped the wrath of Barre's regime during the civil war. Hargeysa was not as lucky. Barre's armies ransacked the city. Many residents, including my sister Amina, lost everything, including reminders of births, weddings, and other treasured social events.

I wanted to help my relation rebuild a family memorabilia collection, so after the Somaliland trip, I rummaged through my photo archives. My hopes of finding something valuable soared when I saw an envelope dated 1984. That was the date of my last trip to the Somali Republic.

The envelope contained photographs of my sister Amina's first-born infant, Axmed. He was barely five months old and was sitting on his father's lap in Mogadishu. Today, he is a lawyer and a member of the Somaliland Parliament. I digitised the photos and mailed them to Amina. She instantly sent back a recorded message in a trembling voice.

"Walaal Ilaalhay haku daayo. Waad naga farxisey markaad soo saartey taariikh naga luntey markii Hargeysa laga qaxay." *Brother, may Allah give you a long life. You made us happy when you discovered things we lost when we fled Hargeysa.*

On another occasion, I visited a relative in Hargeysa whose father had an impressive library of photographs and videos.

"Maxamed, can I see some of your father's photos?" I asked.

"Gone," he replied glumly.

I had no words for the loss he had just reported. After a long pause, Maxamed left the room and returned with a handbag with a faded label.

"This is all I have got," he said with downcast eyes.

I poked a hand inside. I found black-and-white negatives and a dozen or so 8-millimetre movie rolls. The rolls had a Kodak insignia and Arabic squiggles. The handwriting was unmistakably Xaaji Yuusuf Iman's.

Maxamed had rescued them at the peak of the civil war. He held on to them for over thirty years. No one else had seen the stash.

Xaaji Yuusuf was an avid photographer, a businessman, and a politician. Between his frequent travels, he entertained his children and others in his care with silent movies. Most of Xaaji Yuusuf 's archives in Hargeysa and Mogadishu vanished at the height of the civil war.

"Take good care of this," Maxamed said when he handed over his treasure bag to me.

"Waayahay adeer," I reassured him. *OK, my nephew.*

I delivered the package to a studio agent in Johannesburg, South Africa, for restoration. In a month, the agent rewarded us with clips of Somaliland's independence. One clip had footage of local dignitaries flying to London to discuss Somaliland's roadmap to autonomy with the Colonial Office. People lined the roadsides. Those at the airport jubilantly waved flags. There were other clips of the Gulaid family, including several photos of myself. I was about twelve or fourteen years old. One astonishing discovery unveiled itself on the reel jackets. Several bore postage stamps celebrating the independence of Somaliland on 26 June 1960.

I sent digital copies of the negatives and video clips to my relative in Hargeysa. The photos were of a different world, an era of optimism and peace in the Somali Republic, but the material was also a reminder of another casualty of war: the extensive loss and the speed with which it occurred, unsettling. People, institutions, and memorabilia – the sorrowful list goes on and on.

After Sheekh and Hargeysa, I saw another example of amnesia in this Cadaadley, a scene of a stunning SNM victory against Barre's regime.

Cadaadley is thirty kilometres west of Gacan Libaax Mountain. It has no industry, no good roads, and no electricity. The only school there has not recovered from the clashes when Barre's army turned it into a command centre in 1988. The village does have, however, two togs – Cadaadely and Siig. The togs nurture the hand-dug wells that have sustained nomads in the area for centuries.

Cadaadley's modern claim to fame comes from its location. It sits at the geographic centre of the three largest towns in Somaliland – Hargeysa, Berbera, and Burco. If you drive from the village in any direction, you cross a vital road in less than an hour.

The British saw the strategic value of the place and established a military camp there. The Somali Republic turned the area into a base for its elite commando troops at independence.

SNM fighters captured Cadaadley on 29 May 1988. My brother, Xuseen Dheere, was the overall commander of this SNM force. I wanted to see a place that was important during Somaliland's struggle against Barre's regime. My brother Max arranged a trip. We left his farm one morning on a Land Cruiser on rough roads and reached Cadaadley in less than an hour.

We approached the village from the south as the SNM forces had. Our vehicle followed a dirt track winding through the town. We followed a northeasterly direction in the hopes of finding the old military barracks.

The driver and I searched for prominent markers.

The old tracks to the camp had faded. Rain and water runoff had done a remarkable job. Thus, we drove randomly on the hillside, pausing and scanning for signs of an old settlement. There were none.

We doubled back on our route twice and started the search over again. Ultimately, we reached a clearing the size of a football field. We moved close and saw three cement blocks less than two metres tall, probably old structures for training soldiers.

Behind the concrete structures, we saw a crumbling acacia fence. It made the place look like a large animal shed that Somali herders use for livestock. There were no gates or flagpoles. The site was ghostly silent.

I pressed the driver to go around the camp; he obliged. Then I changed my mind and jumped out of the car halfway around the base, preferring to explore the place on foot. I saw several crumbled buildings about 300 metres away. The rubble piles differed in size. I made out broken clay bricks but did not see roofing sheets or materials for windows or doors. Amid the rubble stood one solid structure with freshly painted walls gleaming in the glare of the mid-morning sun. It was probably a mosque.

I considered breaching the fence, but my companions discouraged me. We would get in trouble with the police, they said, so I took many pictures of the site from a distance with a telephoto lens.

Then I weaved through the vegetation growing around the camp perimeter, not entirely avoiding contact with the ubiquitous thorny bushes and prickly pears. The reward of this careless navigation emerged later when I boarded the car. I felt a burning sensation from my knees to my toes. That was a new experience for me, but our driver diagnosed it instantly.

"It's the hair-like thorns of the prickly pears in your socks and trousers," he said.

The darn things were invisible. I tried to resist the urge to fuss while touring this hallowed ground, but my fingers moved up and down my legs, rubbing them and occasionally scraping off some skin.

No matter. My head was in another space, trying to make sense of the scene and manage the questions whirling inside. What was the story of the camp? How did one explain the glaring neglect of historical sites? Is amnesia developing in a nation that sacrificed so much for a struggle against a military tyrant?

There was not even a plaque to honour the men who fell on 29 May 1988 and those who risked their lives to fight the forces of tyranny.

I recalled the words of Teju Cole, a Nigerian American writer and photographer, after viewing a poor exhibit of Nigeria's glorious artefacts at the National Museum in Lagos.

"What, I wonder, is the social consequence of life in a country that has no use for history?"

In Hargeysa, my nephew Axmed consoled me when he heard of my disappointment. He organised a luncheon with SNM veterans of the Cadaadley battle: Axmed Weysacade, Yuusuf Maydal, and Saleybaan Cisman Shide. Axmed and Yuusuf were unit leaders at the battle. Saleybaan was a paratrooper. Over lunch, I heard synopses of the fight.

"Odayaal, maantaa idinweydiin maayo walaalkey Xuseen Dheere, ninkii watay ciidankii SNM ee Cadaadley weerarey. Waxaan jeclahay inaan ogaado sida koox yar oo SNM ahi uga guulestey cidankii weeynaa ee xooga badnaa ee fadhiyey Cadaadley," I said. *Gentlemen, my interest today is not about my brother and your leader, Xuseen Dheere. I want to know how a small guerrilla force overcame the large, better-equipped government forces.*

"We can only tell you things as we saw them," said one veteran at the start of our conversation. "And don't worry if some of the information you hear differs slightly from what you heard from other sources."

I dismissed the caveat and continued scribbling notes on the salient elements of the operation – the attack, response, counteraction, and morale of the SNM fighters.

As the veterans spoke, other hotel customers instantly drifted over to our table to greet them. When I saw the stream of uninvited guests, my nephew and I shifted the group to a quiet corner. A young waiter moved our team to a small gazebo-like room. The walls muffled our conversation and spared us the interruption of men wanting to rub shoulders with this distinguished group.

The war veterans then shared an account of the battle for Cadaadley for over two hours.

"We struck the Cadaadley in the early evening of May 29th, 1988," said one veteran.

"We had two targets," said another. "The barracks just north of the village and the Cadaadley school, which Barre's troops turned into the Command-and-Control Centre."

"Both targets fell quickly. Barre's forces regrouped and launched a counter-offensive the next day. We beat them again."

"How many casualties did you have?"

"Very low. About six deaths on the first day," said another veteran.

Saleybaan, who trained in the camp, resolved my query about the perimeter. "The place had a wall about 1.65 metres high," he said.

They said the Cadaadley victory would not have come without a considerable risk (*miidaamin*), battle-hardened fighters, or deep faith in the struggle against Barre. They eschewed reference to individual heroism as a factor in their victory but remembered to say that the SNM commanders had worked well together.

I saw something that day in the unplanned mixing of veterans and hotel clients – people truly admired these veterans of the struggle. Yet, of the three at our lunch, not one maintained a high post in government or had converted fame to material wealth.

I profusely thanked the men but felt sad we had so little time to discuss that complex operation and the courage of the SNM force that had captured the commando base in 1988; however, I reminded them that it was essential to keep the memories of that struggle alive.

"A national flag or a plaque in Cadaadley will go a long way in honouring the veterans of the struggle and their sacrifices," I said as we bid goodbye.

Hopefully, Yuusuf, one of the leaders of the SNM Veterans Association, would push for memorials to honour that historic struggle against Barre's despotic rule.

The Cadaadley Operation was vital in the Somaliland struggle. It neutralised Barre's elite troops and captured arms, vehicles, and fuel. The fall of Cadaadley meant Barre's government had lost a strategic base. From this camp, the SNM sent reinforcements to other places as needed. One SNM unit backed the SNM contingent in Burco. Another contingent rushed to Hargeysa, where SNM forces battled massive government troops.

Muuse Biixi, an SNM commander who is now the president of Somaliland, said in a video interview with Maxamuud Cabdi Ducaale of Horn Cable TV, "Madaxdii oo dhan way ku dhaawacmeen dagaalkii Hargeysa aniga mooye. Xuseen Dheere aya nooga soo gurmaday Cadaadley." *All the officers [of SNM] except me sustained injuries in the battle for Hargeysa in 1988. Xuseen rushed from Cadaadley to help out.*

Mandheera is another historical place in the struggle against Barre's dictatorship in Somaliland. It had surprises for us. From Cadaadley we travelled north on a gravel road. The dirt track ran on a ridge until we reached Il Carmo, where the Golis range drops precipitously. The four-by-four cruised in the first fifteen minutes of the ride but started to jolt sideways as the driver negotiated the rugged five-kilometre path through the Jarato Pass.

We passed the ruins of old Mandheera before entering the new sections of town. The infamous prison sat by the roadside on the farthest point south of the new settlement.

I wanted pictures, so I stopped our driver and trained a camera with a telescopic lens on the compound about 200 metres away. From my vantage point, I could see the prison walls to my left, the tog, and the hills on the right-hand side of the prison gate. The two places were about 300 to 400 metres apart. Standing there, I appreciated the genius of Colonel Lixle, the mastermind of the plan to rescue Barre's hostages in 1983. He had selected a convenient escape route for the freed prisoners and the SNM attack unit.

While setting up my camera, I heard someone hollering. It was a man wearing a white undershirt, a macawis, and flip-flops. He stood by an old sedan with the driver's door open.

"Maxaad sameeyneesaan?" he asked. *What are you doing?*

Unsure of his intentions, I ignored his first call.

"Waryaa, maxaad u sawiireeysaan meeshan?" *Hey, you, why are you taking pictures of the place?*

"Meeshan taariikhiga ayaan sawiranayaa. Maanan arag digniin odhaneeysaa sawir ha qaadin." *I want a picture of this historic place, and I did not see a sign prohibiting photography.*

"Waar waa mamnuuc. Jooji hadadan." *Photographs are not allowed. Stop right now.*

"Safar dheer ayaanu soo galney siaanu usiyaarano goobaha taariikhiiga ah. Mida kale, nimnakii meesha xoreeyey ehelkoodaan nahay. Miyaad na eryeeysaa?" *We have come a long way to see this historic place. Also, we are related to some of the men who liberated this area from Barre's regime. Would you drive us away?*

"Waar kumaad aheeyd." *Tell me who are you.*

"Xuseen Dheere walaalkii." *Brother of Xuseen Dheere.*

"Waar laisuma ogola sawirka. Bal waxaad yeeshaa, laba sawir oo jeelka ah iyo intaad doonto oo buraha ah kagaadhsiiyoo oo socoda." *Photography is not allowed. Take two shots of the prison quickly and all the shots you want of the hills and move on.*

"Mahadsanid." *Thank you.*

I followed the advice and returned to the vehicle. We drove off with a veil of chalky dust trailing us. In that haze, I wondered about the correctional officer's reaction to the camera. Perhaps the SNM's record of successful prison raids had exposed the vulnerability of the local prison system and was keeping such people on their toes. I wondered if everyone taking the Jarato route was now a suspect.

Invisible State

Somaliland is the size of the State of Connecticut in the USA and as populous. The country gained independence a month before I landed there to attend school. I was too young to grasp the significance of the political change, but I remember seeing the tell-tale signs of a party I had just missed – flags, banners, and colourful lights on streets and buildings and the broadcast of catchy songs on Radio Hargeysa.

What were my parents thinking? I often wondered. My answer as an adult is that they believed Somaliland had entered a new era. They placed higher hopes in their ancestorial land than in Isiolo, where colonial laws crippled movement, trade, and employment for Somalis no longer needed to fight colonial wars. Why else would they send a child to a place 2,000 kilometres away?

Early in our lives, the country and I needed proper guidance. My mentors were dedicated but poorly paid teachers living in rural areas. I fondly remember Macalin (teacher) Ismail, Qowdan, and Abdi in elementary school. At the intermediate level, there were six Somali teachers (Jama, Suleiman, Lumumba, Tahir, Adan, and Mohamed), two Peace Corps volunteers (Butch and Paul), and one Egyptian volunteer (Mohamed).

In secondary school, there was one Somali (Ahmed), an Irishman (McKinley), two Englishmen (Darlington and Feiler), and three Indians (Daniel, Elias, and Singh).

These men taught me languages, history, geography, sciences, and mathematics. They seldom missed class and consistently modelled values I cherish today – honesty, hard work, and service – things I can never forget.

For Somaliland, the stewardship initially fell on politicians. This arrangement ended abruptly when army officers deposed the civilian government and appointed themselves as guardians of the Somali nation. I was a sophomore in secondary school then.

The military era lasted twenty-two years. It began with many promises, an intense media drive, a literacy campaign, and militarisation. Then came the creation of the Stasi-style (East German) police system, repressive policies, and the rollout of interventions that permanently scarred the nation.

General Barre frequently lectured the nation on the merits of scientific socialism and other topics. When he paused, praise singers took to the air to shower him with accolades. In short order, Barre acquired impressive epithets such as The Father of Knowledge and the Bearer of Victories. In reality, Barre had limited formal education. He also squandered a tangible victory during the Ogaden War between Somalia and Ethiopia.

Barre did not win the minds of a fiercely independent people. As a high school student, I, too, had no patience for the rhetoric of scientific socialism. My favourite entertainment came from teashops, which played songs by "underground" songwriters. I still remember the lyrics of popular songs but nothing of the rants of Barre and his lieutenants. Maxamed Ibraahin (Hadraawi), for instance, wrote:

Dadka ha iskaweyneyn
Inaad keli wax garad tahay
Ha iskadhigin walaale.
Stop thinking of yourself as the greatest
And, brother, don't pretend
You know it all.

Also, Cabdillahi Qarshe, a renowned songwriter who promoted nationalism, wrote:

Dadkan dhawaaqayaa
Dalkooda doonayaa
Hadey udhidhiyeen
Alahayow u dhiib.

Those raising their voices
Those seeking self-determination
If they work hard for the cause
Allah, grant them their wish.

The lyrics of another song went like this:

Soomaliyeey toosey toosoo isku tiirsadey
Hadba kiina taag daraneeyn
Ttaagera weligiiney.

Awake Somalis
Awake and lean on each other
The weakest, the vulnerable among you
Help them always.

I completed my secondary education months before the third anniversary of the military takeover in Somalia. Then I went to Kenya with a small suitcase and a newly minted high school certificate. This decision saved me from the drudgery of boot camp, which Barre's government had just imposed on all high school graduates, but returning had its surprises.

I reached Isiolo five years after the cessation of territorial hostilities between Kenya and the Somali Republic. Isiolo, one of the contested districts, had changed. Livestock, the mainstay of the local economy, had vanished. My family, which had owned one of the largest herds of livestock before the conflict, didn't have a goat. Many Isiolo residents sought refuge in Somalia and Tanzania.

I wandered into my village looking for advice but could not find anyone with influence or familiarity with the pathways to higher education.

I was getting discouraged, but my hopes revived when a distant relative introduced me to Abdilahi Haji, an American-educated Somali Kenyan living in Nairobi. Abdilahi took me under his wing, gave me my first job, sent me for a crash course on tourism at the Kenya Institute of Administration, and introduced me to his alma mater in the United States. Three years later, I travelled to Connecticut to attend Trinity College on a scholarship.

As my good fortune continued, the young republic of Somalia withered under the yoke of the military junta. Yet I persisted and found ample encouragement and learning opportunities at various stops, and I regularly followed news about the relatives and school friends I had left behind.

A severe famine wiped out about twenty-five per cent of the nomads' livestock between 1973 and 1974. A war with Ethiopia displaced nearly a million inhabitants from Ogaden in 1977-1978. Residents of northern Somalia (now Somaliland) suffered neglect and marginalisation.

The situation in the Somali Republic worsened in the late 1980s. Random arrests of poets, businessmen, clergy, and youth increased. So did the persecution of Northerners. In response, several movements emerged to confront the regime. The rebellion escalated, and Barre lost power in 1991. In the same year, the thirty-one-year union of Somaliland and Somalia ended acrimoniously.

Over two decades, the military ruler of the Somali Republic controlled all the levers of power in the country. He had opportunities to guide a young nation and lay the foundations for tolerance, democracy, and development, but Barre and his lieutenants could not match the legacy of the teachers who mentored my generation of students. Under Barre's watch, the Somali Republic collapsed.

On my return to Hargeysa in 2019, the union of Somaliland and Somalia had been dead for nearly thirty years. A tri-coloured flag fluttered on poles previously reserved for the blue union flag. More than anything else, this symbol reminded me of the profound change that had taken place.

Yet, political legitimacy has remained elusive even though Somaliland has better human rights records and political freedoms than many other nations that enjoy international political recognition.

Why has Somaliland not received the attention it deserves? I pored over the literature but did not find a valid justification; however, there is evidence that external forces on local affairs provided a critical influence.

Once a British protectorate, Somaliland gained independence from Britain on 26 June 1960. On that occasion, congratulatory messages, including those from the Queen of England and the US Secretary of State who sent notes to Somaliland's Prime Minister Maxamed Ibraahin Cigaal, poured in from around the world. In addition, thirty-four UN member states, including the United Kingdom, the United States, the USSR, Israel, Egypt, France, and Ghana, promptly recognised Somaliland. Many people have forgotten this history.

Somaliland left the union with Italian Somalia in 1991. Yet, Maxamed Ibraahim Cigaal met indifference when he returned as the president. Somaliland has had three other presidents, all democratically elected, and they received the same treatment.

Why the indifference? Two factors come to mind. One is the outlook of global powers. Another is the conduct of the AU.

Historical records show that powerful nations prioritise their strategic interests. For the United States, the containment of Communism was its primary concern for decades. To that end, the US military established a sophisticated communications base (Kagnew) in Asmara, Eritrea, in 1943. It used this facility to monitor communist activities in the Middle East, the Red Sea, and the Indian Ocean. In exchange for the use of this facility, the US government provided military and economic aid to Ethiopia. It also looked the other way as Ethiopia first drew Eritrea into a federation and annexed it in 1962. The United States left Asmara in 1973.

By 1977, Communism had made inroads in Ethiopia, and a nationalist movement was ascending in Eritrea. The United States closed Kagnew and opened a new base in Diago Garcia, a British island in the Indian Ocean.

The United States' influence in the Horn of Africa markedly declined. At that time, the Soviet flag flew high in the Ethiopian and Somali capitals. Then Barre flipped sides after quarrelling with his benefactors in Moscow. He was unhappy with the Soviet alliance with Ethiopia, Somalia's arch-rival in the Horn of Africa. Barre, however, remained on good terms with the United States until his ouster.

In 1982, General Barre shed his military fatigues and visited the USA. He met President Ronald Reagan at the White House and walked away with military and economic aid. American backing for the dictator continued long after Amnesty International published its account of Barre's atrocities in northern Somalia.

"Barre had an image problem," someone decided, so the State Department hired Paul Manafort to embellish the dictator's image in 1989. This assignment fell on Riva Levinson, one of Manafort's young aides. Manafort was Ronald Regan's campaign manager.

Recounting her story as a Manafort aide to *The Washington Post* in 2017, Levinson wrote:

"I told Manafort it didn't seem like a promising strategy to march into a murderous dictator's office and point out to him and his lieutenants that he had a public relations problem. 'Are we sure we want this guy as a client?' I asked.

Manafort replied: 'We all know Barre is a bad guy, Riva. We just have to make sure he's our bad guy. Have a great trip!'"

Manafort, once a deal maker in Washington, DC, fell from grace. In 2018, he cheated his country and went to jail for money laundering, tax fraud, and illegal lobbying.

After the collapse of the Soviet Union, the United States embraced counterterrorism as a flagship agenda. In 2006, Washington waged a proxy war against the Union of Islamic Courts (UIC), a Mogadishu-based militia group fighting against the alliance of warlords. Ethiopian forces invaded southern Somalia with US backing, captured Mogadishu, and removed the UIC from the national capital.

The single issue-driven US foreign policy has had limited success. The strategy did not prepare the Horn for democracy or keep the Soviets out in the 1970s. Moreover, the US proxy war against the UIC had unintended repercussions. It dislodged UIC control in Mogadishu but inspired the Al-Shabaab movement. Since then, counterterrorism has been the primary US foreign policy objective in Somalia.

Dr Jendayi Frazer, the Under Secretary for Africa in the Obama administration, was at a panel discussion at Harvard University in April 2021. She said she had one regret from her years in office: not pushing for Somaliland's recognition.

For Britain, the draw to the Somali Republic is its untapped riches, especially its offshore oil and gas. Sir Michael Howard was likely a key proponent of ensuring access to Somali resources. He was the chair of Soma Oil and, coincidentally, a former chair of the Conservative Party.

Soma Oil and others with commercial interests in the Somali coastline know the political arithmetic well: keep the Mogadishu government happy even if this effort meant British neglect of Somaliland.

Since the creation of Soma Oil and Gas in 2013, Britain has upstaged Italy, the former colonial power, as an advocate for Somalia. Two secretaries (William Hague and Boris Johnson) visited Mogadishu in less than a decade. Britain also hosted pledging conferences in London.

Not surprisingly, Soma Oil's conduct has not been above reproach. On 4 August 2015, Reuters published a story with this headline: "UN Monitors Accuse British Oil Firms of Payoffs to Somali Officials." It said, "UN sanctions experts accused Soma Oil and Gas of making large payments to Somalia's oil ministry that created a 'serious conflict of interest,' some of which appeared to have been used to pay off senior officials."

UN monitors described the capacity-building programme as "likely part of a quid pro quo arrangement, whereby the ministry would protect the Somali contract from any negative reviews when a panel chaired by the Somali Ministry of Finance began reviewing all its contracts." The UN statement prompted an investigation by the Serious Fraud Office of the United Kingdom.

Increased British attention in Somalia is unprecedented. Although British people have hosted thousands of Somali refugees, colonial Britain was less generous. Colonial Britain did more to undermine Somali dreams than any other foreign power in the last century.

In 1897, Britain unilaterally bequeathed Somali territories to Emperor Menelik II of Ethiopia. In 1954, Britain ceded Somali grazing land to Ethiopia. In 1963, Britain also thwarted the merger of the NFD with Somalia. Colonial Britain also waged war against a nationalist movement under the leadership of Mohamed Abdule Hassan for twenty years.

Somali grievances do not end there. After the defeat of Italy in World War II, the Italian colony of Somalia was under the British Military Administration for nearly a decade, from 1941 to 1949. During their watch over the former Italian colony, British forces gunned down unarmed protestors agitating for independence. One of the most famous monuments in Mogadishu commemorates the action of the demonstrators. Another monument honours the nationalist Maxamed Cabdule Xasan, who fought the British for decades.

Rich nations seldom talk about their strategic interests in Somalia. At press conferences, they deflect questions on Somaliland. They also like to push the matter to the AU, the regional body with a mandate for peace and reconciliation.

Somaliland reached out to the AU in 2005. Axmed Maxamed Siilaanyo, the third president of Somaliland, was in office. The AU took an important step. It sent a fact-finding mission to Somaliland. Members of the mission concluded their work successfully. They also commented favourably about the country's quest for recognition:

"Despite fears that recognition would lead to the fragmentation of Somalia or other AU member states," the AU mission concluded that the situation was sufficiently "unique and self-justified in African political history" that "the case should not be linked to the notion of 'opening a pandora's box.'" It recommended that the AU "find a special method of dealing with this outstanding case at the earliest possible date." The commission further declared: "The issue cannot be allowed to drag on indefinitely. It must be addressed."

Since the commission made that call, the AU has been silent. Meanwhile, the isolation of Somaliland has continued, and so has the growth of the vulnerable population. Fifteen cohorts of children were born. Of these, nearly 22,000 died from measles alone based on my projections using population statistics and immunisation coverage levels. This tragedy has not elicited appropriate responses.

Meanwhile, Mogadishu has the sole mandate for international affairs concerning Somalia and Somaliland. This approach is problematic for several reasons. Mogadishu officials who make the critical decisions have not set foot in Somaliland for over three decades. Some officials are, in fact, hostile to Somaliland. Maxamed Cabdulahi Maxamed, popularly known as Farmaajo, is an example. He was president of Somalia and the sixth head of state since Barre's ouster in 1991.

Maxamed embraced a sanitised version of the history of the conflict in northern Somalia, now Somaliland. In a master's thesis he submitted to the University at Buffalo (New York) in 2009, he wrote: "The SNM guerrilla army briefly seized two major towns in northern Somalia – Hargeysa and Burco – in 1988. Barre and his superior American weapons reacted by emphatically crushing the SNM movement. He essentially levelled the rebel cities. Many civilians died in the crossfire; thousands more fled for the countryside, where water and shelter were short."

Maxamed was silent on the state-sponsored violence, deployment of mercenaries in the destruction of Hargeysa, and the role of the Somali Air Force in the bombardment of Somalia's second-largest city and the strafing of civilians.

As president, Maxamed's administration adopted aggressive policies towards Somaliland. In 2019, Somalia wrested control of the airspace of the two countries from the International Civil Aviation Organisation. This intervention meant scrapping a previous plan that supported a joint regulatory body and sharing revenue accrued from overflights. Maxamed's administration also scuttled agreements that his predecessors had reached as part of the Somaliland-Somalia talks.

Maxamed's most recent action came late in his tenure. In June 2020, he broached the most sensitive topic in Somaliland-Somalia relations with a speech focused on the decades of ill-treatment of Northerners and the destruction of their cities. For this reason alone, the initiative received considerable attention and, indeed, made history.

I replayed the video of Maxamed's speech several times to be sure I did not miss anything. I was sorely disappointed. I heard a half-hearted apology. He chose words like "difficulties" and "wrongs" to refer to atrocities, and his concluding remarks dispelled any doubts I had about the sincerity of the apology.

"Truly, what happened there was not a Southern attack on the North. It was not part of a clan activity ... It was an act of the government system that existed at that time," he said.

A United Nations report paints a different picture: "Based on the totality of evidence collected in Somaliland and elsewhere both during and after the mission, the consultant firmly believes that the crime of genocide was conceived, planned, and perpetrated by the Somali Government against the Isaac people of Northern Somalia between 1987 and 1989."

Maxamed took a bold step that deserves commendation for approaching a critical topic that had eluded most of his predecessors. Regrettably, however, Maxamed retreated when he had the attention of a deeply fractured society. At best, Maxamed tended to skimp on the facts. At worst, he absolved Barre of committing crimes against humanity.

Thus, a murky situation prevails. Somaliland remains stateless; decision-makers in Mogadishu dwell in a past when there was a union; the AU is unresponsive; and mighty nations hedge their bets on recognising Somaliland. Joshua Keating, a foreign policy analyst, has a penetrating observation about the country's predicament: "Somaliland's main obstacle is not the world's animosity, but its indifference," he wrote in the *Guardian* in 2018. I saw first-hand the consequences of this policy.

Because of Somaliland's status, children face more uncertainties today than when I started school in 1960. Regarding child survival, Somaliland stands where developing countries were in 1984. The youth, representing nearly seventy-five per cent of the population, languish in the void of statelessness even after attaining higher education at local universities.

For nearly three decades, this population has shown remarkable discipline. They have eschewed the two most potent urges for people their ages: illegal migration and terrorism. It is hard to say how long their discipline will hold, but the West will complain about illegal migration if their patience runs out, and some countries will readily deploy drones and counter-insurgency troops if there is a hint of radicalisation among the youth.

My trip convinced me that international indifference to Somaliland is counterproductive. It is time for the AU and Western countries to reward Somaliland's experiment with democracy and its remarkable success in combating terrorism and illegal migration.

Home and the Diaspora

The dispersal of Somalis around the world occurred at an astonishing rate. In the 1980s, there were less than a few hundred Somali souls in the United States. That picture was much the same in the United Kingdom, a popular destination for sailors and graduates of my old secondary school in Sheekh.

Today, there are vibrant Somali communities in North America, Europe, Australia, the Middle East, and East and Southern Africa. My extended family alone hails from Australia, Canada, Germany, Holland, Saudi Arabia, Sweden, the United Kingdom, and the United States.

Between 1979 and 1983, I was the only ethnic Somali in Minnesota; in 2019, according to a CBS-affiliated radio station, there were 69,000 Somalis there. Among them are my son, nephews, nieces, cousins, and schoolmates from Sheekh. Caasha, one of my grandnieces, briefly taught at the University of Minnesota School of Medicine. She left the university for a job with the Mayo Clinic. My son is a nurse at the Fairview Hospital, and one of my nephews is a diligent truck driver in the state.

Another niece, whom I had not seen since she finished high school in Upstate New York, recently showed up in Nairobi. She is the chief medical officer for the United States diplomatic staff in East Africa, specialising in emergency medicine. In her thirties, she had the unenviable task of overseeing a team that catered to the US diplomatic community during the first year of the COVID-19 epidemic.

Indeed, my Somali family is far-reaching. In 2018, for instance, I spent three months in Ukraine as the UNICEF interim head. Soon after landing in Kyiv, I immersed myself in children's affairs in a country facing economic and military threats from Russia. While there, I travelled to Germany to meet my nephews Axmed, Cabdula, and Libaan. They are the offspring of my brother Hussein, a veteran of the anti-Barre movement in Somaliland. I had never met them although my brother Max and I had contributed to their upkeep since my brother died in 2003. My American wife took on this African-style social welfare system and managed to transfer a subsistence allowance to the family every month. Over sixteen years, she never missed a single payment.

These nephews joined the waves of young people leaving Somalia after the civil war. They crossed the frontiers and ended up in Germany. A reunion was long overdue. Besides getting acquainted, I wanted to give them fatherly advice and a pep talk about living overseas. Such conversation is typical among Somalis.

Over the two-day visit, I enjoyed the company of my three handsome nephews. Cabdula and Libaan had short, trimmed beards. They wore fashionable clothes and haircuts. We chatted and feasted together for two days. They also gave me a Lubeck tour and posted a picture of our reunion at the famous Holsten Gate on Facebook.

At Axmed's home, we pampered his children, a four-year-old girl and an infant boy. The baby clung to his parents. His sister was different. She moved from one uncle's lap to another and made funny faces if I pointed my phone camera at her. She would not leave my side on day two but did not complain when I left the house with her father and uncles.

I watched the next generation of the Gulaids, victims of the war in Somalia, settling in Germany. Happy with my nephews' fresh start in life, I wondered how far they would go.

I addressed them after a feast at a Turkish restaurant. I reminded them of their struggles to get to where they were and the sacrifices of older generations.

"You now have a new home, right?"

"Yes, Uncle," they said.

"Respect your country. And don't squander the opportunities you have."

"We hear you, Uncle."

Gulaid, a fourth sibling of the fellows in Germany, lived in a neighbouring country. His adventure began in Eastern Ukraine where he enrolled at a university. After the pro-Russian militia invaded Eastern Ukraine, he joined the people fleeing the conflict and settled in Kyiv. Various organisations helped Gulaid and other displaced people. One NGO hired him because they liked his communication skills. He served as a Kyiv caseworker, interpreter, and organiser for five years. When the international refugee resettlement began, Gulaid and his family were accepted in Sweden. As such, Gulaid could not join us because he was busy with his refugee induction programme in Stockholm, but he called us several times.

"Uncle, I wish I was in Kyiv with you. I could have shown you around or interpreted for you," he said.

"Thank you, nephew," I said. "My problem is not the language; it's the freezing weather." I did not mention my six-year stint in Minneapolis in my youth.

Gulaid laughed and then adopted a more serious tone.

"Uncle, I have a family but married someone from a distant tribe."

It was my turn to laugh. "You call a marriage to a Somali distant? Look at me. My wife, who sent the subsistence allowance to families in Hargeysa for sixteen years, is an American. You're fine if you marry the woman you love."

I spared him stories of failed marriages among Somali men and women with close kinship ties.

"Thank you, Uncle," Gulaid said.

On the flight back to Kyiv, I replayed scenes of the encounter with my nephews in my head. Beyond the frequent posting of selfies on Facebook, I knew they were resilient and determined. These skills helped them survive Barre's turmoil, navigate the treacherous routes to the heart of Europe, and make a home in a new land. And to be sure, there are also talents yet unexplored among the Somalis in the diaspora.

Britain did not wait long to realise the talent of its Somali immigrants. Mo Farah, a slender Somali immigrant, became a British legend during the 2012 Summer Olympics in London. He won two gold medals. The roar of the British crowd cheering him on in the stadium reverberated across the kingdom. Farah won the gold medal again in the 5,000- and 10,000-metre races at the Rio de Janeiro Olympic Games in 2016.

The United Kingdom, with its rich history of athletic accomplishments, had never excelled like this in track and field. For his achievements, Farah was awarded the Commander of the Order of the British Empire (CBE) in 2013 and was knighted five years later.

Somalis have given Sweden its first top-rated R&B (rhythm and blues) singer and songwriter. She is Shiriihan Maxamed Cabdile, whose stage name is Cherrie.

Cherrie was born in Oslo, Norway, in 1991. She spent her early years in Finland before settling in Sweden. Cherrie swept the country like a storm out of Rinkeby, the neighbourhood in Stockholm with the largest immigrant population. *Vogue* magazine described her as a "Somali-Swedish R&B queen with style and substance."

Britain has Warsan Shire, a poet. The *New York Times* described her as "the woman who gave poetry to Beyoncé's *Lemonade*, an award-winning album.

Axmed Ismail is another Somali immigrant to the United Kingdom who has made a name for himself in finance. He fled Somaliland in 1988 and found asylum in the United Kingdom where he studied economics. Ismail did odd jobs as a student. Motivated to solve immigrants' challenges with sending remittances to relatives left behind, he co-founded WorldRemit in 2010. WorldRemit is a top-notch money transfer firm that services 150 countries worldwide today. In 2019, Ismail topped the 100 Most Influential Black Britons list.

In politics, Somalis stand out among fellow immigrants for their engagement. Ilhan Omar became one of two Muslim women to serve in the US Congress. In 2021, she handily won re-election despite a sustained assault from former US President Donald Trump and far-right political groups in the USA.

In Canada, Axmed Xuseen became the Minister of Immigration and Citizenship in 2017 in Justin Trudeau's government. Axmed immigrated to Canada in 1993 and studied law. He also earned the Queen's Gold Medal for leadership efforts in the Regent Park community in Toronto.

Sada Mire is a Swedish-Somali archaeologist, an art historian, and a lecturer at Leiden University in Holland. She has explored the archaeological riches of Somaliland, which had remained hidden for millennia. The Hay Festival of Literature and the Arts selected Mire as one of its thirty international thinkers and writers in 2017.

My examples depict the achievements of a sample of early achievers. Undoubtedly, there are many individuals with glowing résumés in the diaspora. And I am confident Somalis will prosper in the "Warmth of the Other Suns," as Richard Wright, a famous Black writer said of African Americans escaping oppression in the American South.

However, the diaspora community has its challenges. Two issues of significance to Somaliland are the dwindling elderly population and the loyalty to tribalism.

The elderly population is shrinking, and sadly, the COVID-19 epidemic has disproportionately affected the elderly Somali community, especially in Europe. This trend is worrying because the older Somalis in the diaspora play a vital role in community relations and knowledge transfer. They orient younger generations, bridge cultures, and manage remittances to relatives left behind.

Second, loyalty to tribalism is prominent among the Somalis in the diaspora. No other force poses a more significant threat to the advancement of Somali communities there – not the freezing winters of the North and not competition in various fields of endeavour.

The diaspora Somalis, especially the youth, should take note of these factors. They will do well if they keep ties with their homeland and tackle the negative influences of clan loyalty.

They may draw lessons from other societies separated by geography, such as Jews and Koreans.

They must also urgently address the negative influence of campaign financing. This system supports politicians who place clan interests above public welfare. The Somali diaspora will become a force for positive change by addressing these issues.

Awakening

I learnt about Somali Weyn, the national vision, when I started school in 1960. National commitment to this vision was unmistakable. It was on every tongue. The flag with a five-pointed star adorned buildings and streets. Each point denoted one of the Somali-inhabited territories in the Horn of Africa: the former British Somaliland, Italian Somalia, French Somaliland, the NFD of Kenya, and the Ogaden region in Ethiopia.

I fully embraced the idea. I sang nationalist songs, marched with students, and prayed for national success. My outlook changed as an adult when I discovered contradictions. An example is the tension between the Somali Weyn and the core Organisation of African Unity (OAU) principles.

The president of Mali, Madibo Keita, clearly spelt out one core principle at the first OAU meeting in 1963. "We must take Africa as it is; we must renounce territorial claims."

Keita's message received near-universal endorsement. There were a few sceptics – Morocco, Ghana, and the Somali Republic. Morocco claimed the Western Sahara. Ghana wanted Togo. The Somali Republic had its eyes on the NFD of Kenya, the Somali region of Ethiopia, and Djibouti.

Ghana backed down. Morocco stayed relatively quiet. The Somali Republic, though, remained adamant. From then on, Somalia was on a collision course with its neighbours.

In 1963, political tensions erupted in my birth country over the future of the NFD. As Kenya's independence approached, Somali and other communities in the NFD agitated for a say in their futures. Britain, the colonial government, proposed a referendum. People went to polling stations and overwhelmingly voted for a union with the Somali Republic.

Then the unexpected happened. The colonial government disregarded the outcome of the vote. Britain expressly handed over a problem it had already hatched to Kenya's leaders just a few months before they took office.

Kenya's political leaders were unhappy. They launched a campaign to crush the Somali drive for secession. The intervention did not end there. The new government declared an emergency law in NFD. This treatment lasted many years. Britain gave military and economic aid to the fledgling nation of Kenya. The intervention left the NFD impoverished. To this day, districts in the former NFD have some of the lowest development indicators.

This chapter of Kenya's history is not well documented, but a fuller picture of the conflict is slowly emerging. Hannah Whittaker, a professor of modern history at Brunel University, London, pointed out similarities between Kenya's counter-insurgency measures in the NFD and British actions during the Mau Mau era. Collective punishment and forced villagisation are examples. Information presented to Kenya's Truth and Reconciliation Commissions of 2008 complements Whittaker's observations.

Derek Franklin, a special branch officer in the colonial police in Kenya, unwittingly revealed information on British covert activities against Somali nationalists in the NFD. Franklin's service spanned the decades of conflict in Kenya. In his memoir, Mau Mau fighters are presented as "bandits" and Somalis as "shiftas" (thieves). Tracking Kenyan students educated in the Soviet Bloc countries, hunting outlaws, and keeping track of his "kills" were the highlights of his career.

French Somaliland was a strategic place. It was also the terminus of the Franco-Ethiopia rail, which carried much of Ethiopia's imports and exports. For France, the territory was too important to lose, so the colonial government infiltrated the nationalist movement in the colony. Then came the mysterious death of Maxamuud Xarbi, an ardent Somali nationalist, in a plane crash in 1960. The incident had the hallmark of sabotage, possibly by the far-right French terrorist organisation, the Organisation Armée Secrete/Secret Army Organisation (OAS), which sponsored assassinations and attacks on buildings to push for French retention of prized colonies.

On another occasion, France staged a shabby referendum on the colony's future. Critics of the exercise noted that the colonial government manipulated the voter registry, expelling ethnic Somali people who were pro-union with Somalia and granting temporary voting privileges to Afar people brought in from Ethiopia to tip the results in France's favour. France did not stop there. After the vote, it coined a new name for the colony that deleted the reference to Somali. French Somaliland became The French Territory of Afars and Issas.

Djibouti gained independence in 1977. The news triggered fresh celebrations across the Somali regions in the Horn of Africa. However, the celebrations in the Somali Republic were muted because Djibouti snubbed Somali Weyn. Why did Djibouti take this unpopular decision?

A plausible reason was to prevent a possible war between Ethiopia and Somalia over its territory because both neighbours had staked a claim on the territory. Thus, the leaders of Djibouti decided to stand alone, forfeiting a guaranteed seat in the union government of Somalia.

There was another reason just as valid and convincing. Djibouti's leaders must have studied the seventeen-year-old Somali experiment with unification. They probably did not like what they saw. Somaliland became the junior partner in the union. The civilian government in Mogadishu neglected that part of the country. The military deepened the isolation. It also added a heavy dose of violence.

The Ogaden received considerable Somali attention. In 1977, Somalia launched a full-scale military offence there. Somali forces and their local allies captured much of the disputed territory. At that critical moment, Barre alienated the Soviet Union, Somalia's most reliable military ally. In retaliation, Moscow airlifted massive quantities of weapons, Cuban troops, East German advisers, and Yemeni fighters to Ethiopia. With these reinforcements, Ethiopia beat the Somali forces and regained control of all the occupied land. The OAU sided with Ethiopia. Fidel Castro used the OAU's territorial sanctity clause as a pretext for Cuba's assistance in the intervention.

After the Ogaden fiasco, Barre, the custodian of Somali Weyn, turned on his people. First, he attacked the northeastern part of Somalia, now Puntland. The Somali forces killed civilians, raped women, destroyed properties, and poisoned wells in the arid land. Barre's next target was the northwestern part of Somalia, now Somaliland. He unleashed the full might of the Somali Armed Forces. The Somali Air Force dropped bombs on Hargeysa and Burco and strafed civilians. He also hired South African and Rhodesian mercenaries as insurance against any insubordination among Somali pilots asked to drop bombs on fellow citizens.

The human costs of the campaign were high. Roughly 50,000 to 60,000 deaths occurred between May 1988 and the beginning of 1990, according to Africa Watch. The number of displaced people was 400,000 to 500,000. Daniel Compagnon of the World Peace Foundation put the fatalities from the Hargeysa and Burco bombings at 15,000 to 20,000.

Djibouti escaped this pogrom. I could imagine the country's leaders giving thanks to Allah. Had Djibouti voted for membership in Somali Weyn, who knows what the fate of the territory and its people would have been?

In 1988, I completed my graduate studies and two years of work at the Centers for Disease Control and Prevention (CDC) in Atlanta; however, I did not need complex statistical analysis to understand Somalia. The relationship between Somali irredentism and militarisation was glaring. Somalia had added another fatal ingredient to the mix – poor leadership.

This recipe created enduring hardship for Somalis in the Somali Republic and those living on the periphery, notably Ethiopia and Kenya. It also planted the seed for authoritarian rule in the Somali Republic and an adoration of strong men with arms. The violence ultimately caught up with the dictator.

Barre fled Mogadishu and died in exile. His legacy is a failed state, a place with many problems. Buildings have bullet marks. Survivors carry the burden of trauma, both physical and emotional. Hundreds of thousands of children never enjoyed the gift that my generation received at independence – the opportunity to grow up in a safe environment irrespective of clan affinity.

In today's Somalia, the sky-blue flag in Villa Somalia does not carry the aura it once did. Even Mogadishu, the capital of Somali Weyn, relies on international peacekeepers for security.

Now, the blue flag needs a facelift that depicts new aspirations. Mogadishu, once the jewel city in the Indian Ocean, must reinvent itself and compete with other dynamic centres with sizable Somali populations.

I also see the need for atonement and reconciliation for a traumatised society. Such measures could bring much-needed closure to the fraternal feuds, which claimed more victims than all other conflicts put together, including the Ogaden War and the NFD crisis.

In Vietnam, I saw a monument for the victims of the "American War" in nearly every village I visited. Perhaps Somalis should have memorials across the land as reminders of their self-inflicted pain. To each monument, they should inscribe the words "NEVER AGAIN."

On the African Union (AU), I have two observations. The first one is a commendation of its decision to send a fact-finding mission to Somaliland in 2005. The second is a critique due to its lack of follow-up to the urgent recommendations on Somaliland.

The passage of time is remarkable. Some children born when the AU mission was carried out are approaching adulthood. They wonder why the African Union would treat South Sudan and Somaliland differently. The former received speedy attention although South Sudan did not have colonial boundaries. The other met silence, although it has colonial boundaries and had presented to the regional body five years before the AU ratified South Sudan's membership.

Somaliland wants an affirmation and recognition of the sanctity of its colonial boundaries and a seat in the AU like all other countries with a colonial history. AU's indecision on this question prolongs the pain of isolation for an entire nation. It also poses a credibility risk for the regional body if it does not uphold its core principle on colonial boundaries.

Affinity

With the demise of the old Somali dream, I wondered what may hold a once enthusiastic nation together. The phrase *Soomaalinimo* comes to mind.

What is it? Soomaalinimo means the essence of being a Somali or Soomaaliness. It speaks of a sentiment transcending geography, politics, and clan affiliation.

I have seen several expressions of Soomaalinimo. On my first journey to Somalia in 1960, people in towns along the Isiolo-Hargeysa route treated the passengers on our bus as relatives. In 1967, my parents and youngest sister received a friendly reception as refugees from Kenya's former NFD at the Mogadishu International Airport. The reception was so warm that one would think that the Somali Republic had the Israeli Law of Return for people separated by colonial boundaries. They landed at the Mogadishu airport as refugees with one carry-on piece of luggage. No one asked questions.

My third example comes from Helsinki, Finland, where I attended a conference in 1998. Walking on a busy street one day with Ghanaian colleagues, I heard a woman calling out in Somali. "Waa Soomaali! Waa Soomaali!" *A Somali! A Somali!*

She asked in a distinct southern accent, "Brother, are you Somali?"

"Haa." *Yes*, I said and greeted her.

She hugged me. Then she introduced her White male companion as her husband.

"My brother, I haven't seen a Somali for a long time. I feel lost. This man is my husband."

We exchanged a few more words before parting. The woman had a southern accent, and I had a northern one. But that difference did not matter at that moment.

Xidigaha Geeska, a talented group of young artists from Somaliland convey Soomaalinimo in a song called "Afkaygoow qolo matihid." Abwaan Cabdirizaad Xaamud (Jaylaani) wrote it. The song's lyrics are catchy, and the tempo is upbeat, thanks to Maxamed Miyir and Axmedweli Furunli. The message focuses on solidarity among those who share this language.

afkaygoow qolo ma tihid
qabiil iyo reer ma tihid
qof gaar kuu lihi majiro

dadkaaga qaybsamooo
qoloba qolo diidan tahee
adigu waxaa tahay af qudha

aduunkiyo qaaradaha
astaan baad qawm u tahay
qiimaha soomaalinimo
ayaad quwadiisa tahay
afkaygoow ayaad quwadiisa tahay

afkeygoow qaran jiraa tahay
afkeygoow qaali baad tahay
aniga waxaad tahey qudheyda
afkaygoow afkaygoow

afkaygoow qaran jiraa tahay
Jabuuti qiimahaaga weye
Jigjiga quruxdaada weye
Gaarisa qeykaaga weye
Muqdisho qoridaada weye
Hargeysa qaaamuuskaaga weye
Boorama qalinkaaga weye
Bosaaso qiyaastaaada weye

afkaygoow afkaygoow, afkaygoow
aniga waxaa tahay qudhayda

afkaygoow quus ha noqon
kolkay is qardoofayaan
shantii qayb kuu lahayd

qayrkoodbaa kala dilayoo
reer bay isku quudhsadaane
ha moodin inaad qabyowday

qasdiga abuurtee allena
qaybaad dhul ka leedahoo
qorshiyo nolol baad hagtaaye
dunida kuma tihid qaxoontii
afkaygoow afkaygoow

afkaygoow qaran jiraa tahay
afkaygoow qaali baa tahay
aniga waxaa tahay qudhayda
afkaygoow afkaygoow

my language, you don't stand for a tribe
you don't represent a clan or a subclan
no one has a sole dominion over you

Your people are divided
each group dismisses the other
but you are my heartbeat

across the wide world and continents
you are a symbol of a nation
for Soomaaliness
you are the backbone, the pillar
my language, you are its strength

my language, you are the essence of a nation
my language, you are priceless
you are my soul
my language, my language

my language, you are the nation
Djibouti is a source of your pride
Jigjiga is a mirror reflecting your beauty
Garissa is the garment you wear
Mogadishu, the birthplace of your script
Hargeysa is a fountain of knowledge about you
Borama is the home of your scribes
Bossaso is home to those who can measure your worth

my language, my language, my language
you are my soul, my heartbeat

my language, don't despair
when there is discord
among the five [Somali populations] that embrace you

The source of hostilities is peer groups
as one clan belittles the other

but do not feel abandoned

in the creator's overall scheme
you have a place reserved
you inspire plans and dreams
you are not homeless in this world
my language, my language

my language, you are the essence of a nation
you are priceless
you are my soul
my language, my language

• • •

And then there is the story of Axmed Maxamed Xasan, a former pilot of the Somali Air Force and now a Luxembourg citizen. This man took a risk to spare the lives of civilians.

Axmed, better known as Axmed Dheere (tall Axmed), was born in Mogadishu in 1953. He joined the Somali Air Force and trained as a pilot in Egypt and the Soviet Union. He reached the rank of lieutenant colonel.

In early July 1988, Barre's government commanded Colonel Axmed and another Somali officer to fly two MiG-19 planes from the Somali Air Force Base in Bali Doogle, the southern part of Somalia, to Hargeysa. The aircraft refuelled in Gaalkacayo and landed in Hargeysa in the afternoon.

The pilots had a briefing the next day, including information on designated priority targets. At about 10 am the following day, the warplanes took off from Hargeysa, carrying a payload of explosives. In earnest, Barre's war on civilians in Hargeysa had entered a new phase.

Colonel Axmed described what happened next to a youthful audience in Hargeysa in October 2020. I watched a video of that event. Colonel Axmed was the guest, and the audience was comprised primarily of young people. Dr Jaamac Muuse Jaamac, the Hargeysa International Book Fair founder, moderated.

Axmed is a tall fellow with sharp features and a grey beard. His responses to the questions of the moderator and audience were as clear and concise as those of an academic. I liked him instantly.

"What was the target of your mission?" asked Jaamac.

"Anywhere north of the Hargeysa tog," he said.

This zone was the economic and residential hub of the city. The government spared the southwestern side of the riverbed where the 26th Division of the Somali Army kept its base. The airport, from where the aircraft took off, was about ten kilometres southeast of the town.

"How many explosives did your aircraft carry?"

"About 1,000 kilograms. And it took fifteen minutes to drop that load and another fifteen minutes to pick up a new payload."

The two did quick calculations: six or ten runs daily, each payload weighing 1,000 kilograms of explosives, that would come out to 6,000 to 10,000 kilograms.

"What happened next?"

"My aircraft was the second to take off. After gaining a height of 500 metres, I continued climbing instead of making a sharp turn in preparation for a swoop over the designated target."

"Did you receive commands from the control tower?"

"Someone noticed the anomaly in the aircraft route and called me promptly."

"What happened next?"

"I reported a technical problem and switched off the radio. Then I set Djibouti as a destination."

Colonel Axmed executed the secret plan he had conceived a few days earlier. First, he dumped the disarmed payload in an isolated field and headed for Djibouti.

"Weren't you concerned about the command centre sending an aircraft to shoot you down?"

"No. With a head start, I was confident of reaching my destination."

He knew his machine well. The MiG-17 had a maximum cruising speed of 970km/h. It took Axmed no time to reach Djibouti, 245 kilometres northwest of Hargeysa.

Colonel Axmed reported poor visibility that day but reached his destination safely. Running low on fuel, he ditched the plane on a sandy beach near Obok.

The MiG had a high landing speed (about 191 km/h). It required a runway of about 900 metres long with brakes on landing. Luckily, Colonel Axmed escaped injuries during the crash landing.

The French Military Command Centre in Djibouti detected the incursion of an unidentified aircraft. It scrambled two Mirage fighter planes to investigate. They flew over the MiG parked on the isolated beach.

Colonel Axmed extricated himself from the wreckage. He walked about in this lonely corner of Djibouti until he met local fishermen. This group rescued the pilot and handed him over to government officials.

Colonel Axmed met the Minister of Interior a day after entering Djibouti.

"Ku soo dhawaoow Djibouti. Walaaladaa baad amaan gelisey. Anaguna waanu ku amaan gelineeynaa," said the official. *Welcome to Djibouti. You spared your brothers and sisters, and we will do the same.*

To ensure Colonel Axmed's safety, the official handed him over to the United Nations. Colonel Axmed finally found refuge in Luxembourg.

This soldier adopted a unique stance in defence of human rights. He followed his decision at considerable risk to himself. Today, Colonel Axmed is the recipient of the highest national honour, the Medal of Honour. During his 2020 visit to Somaliland, he received a warm welcome. The most extraordinary outpouring I saw came from the youth.

"Markii Hargeysa la duqaynaayey, wax yar baan ahaa. Caraarkii hooyadeey baa dusheey igu qaadey. Hadaad maalintaa duqeeyso magaalada, maanu nabad galeeen. Mahad sanid."

This statement from a young man with a disability translates as follows: I was a baby during the Hargeysa bombing. In the scramble, my mother carried me on her back. If you had dropped bombs that day, I might have been one of the civilian casualties of the raid. I want to thank you for sparing us.

I will provide a final illustration of Soomaalinimo, which occurred on the last days of the 2021 Summer Olympics in Japan. Bashir Abdi of

Belgium and Abdi Negeeye of Holland participated in the marathon race. Many African runners with impressive records were at the starting line. Predicting the winner in this gruelling forty-two-kilometre race at Sapporo was difficult. Everyone had some two hours to wait for a definitive outcome.

An hour in, the field sorted itself out. A lead pack of predominantly African athletes emerged. Among them was the indomitable Eliud Kipchoge of my birth country, Kenya. I convinced myself that an African athlete would almost surely win the race. But who?

In about two hours, Kipchoge crossed the finish line. He defended his title, becoming the third man ever to win gold in this event twice. What a feat, I thought, as I pumped my fists in the air. Soon my attention returned to a story that almost eclipsed this historic achievement. It concerned the race for silver and bronze medals.

Three athletes competed for the honours: Lawrence Chirono of Kenya, Cabdi Negeeye of Holland, and Bashir Cabdi of Belgium. Negeeye and Cabdi are of Somali descent and trained together for this event.

In the final stretch, Cabdi developed a muscle cramp. He gritted his teeth and wobbled on the course. Noticing this, Negeeye slowed down and addressed his training partner.

"Bashir, stay with me!" he shouted.

The finish line was now in sight, but the race was undecided.

Would Negeeye sprint to the tape to secure the silver medal? Would Chirono, a formidable opponent, take advantage of Negeeye's distraction and overtake him?

Negeeye stuck by his friend, urging him to pick up the pace. At this stage, I was on my feet, transmitting positive energy through space to the lame athlete in Japan.

Then something happened. Cabdi revived about fifty metres from the tape. He straightened up and pushed himself to the finishing line.

Negeeye won the silver. Cabdi clinched the bronze. Chirono, the eighth-fastest marathon runner in the world, came fourth.

After the Tokyo race, a journalist asked Negeeye why he had risked his chance for a medal.

Negeeye said, "I knew something was wrong because he [Cabdi] was also a little stronger than me in training and is a good athlete. It was a natural reaction because of our brotherhood and our heritage. We are both Somali."

Somalis around the world celebrated Negeeye's and Cabdi's achievements. Many saw the athletes' triumph as an affirmation of the bond of Soomaalinimo.

Dardaaran

Dardaaran means "parting words" in Somali. A fourth-year medical student at Hargeysa University suggested it. I have four points for him and the other young readers of this story.

First of all, appreciate the value of peace and security. They are Somaliland's most significant achievements, a foundation for everything. Cherish them. Protect them.

If in doubt, ask the thousands of Somalis huddled in Dadaab, the world's largest refugee camp in Kenya, why they have not returned to Somalia. Their answer will revolve around insecurity.

Tribal politics may be the greatest threat to this national asset. A relative in Hargeysa provided this insight on the subject: "Tribalism is the only thing Somalis buried and then exhumed," she said.

I accept her assessment because I witnessed the funeral of this custom and its resurrection. In secondary school, I attended a funeral for tribalism shortly after the military takeover of Somalia in 1969. Barre's government called for rallies to bash tribalism.

I marched with hundreds of students to the commercial centre of Sheekh. Speaker after speaker railed against the evils of tribalism. In the next moment, demonstrators set fire to the effigy of tribalism.

We cheered as fire engulfed the caricature, exclaiming, "Qabyaaladu ha dhacdo." *Down with tribalism.*

The effigy burnt to ashes, but tribalism survived. General Barre adopted it as a guiding philosophy during his rule. Three decades after the collapse of Barre's regime, the spectre of tribal violence remains. The menace will return to Somaliland if leaders pander to tribal whims and the public confounds faith with clan politics. Beware and be vigilant.

Second, give greater attention to the youth. This group represents seventy per cent of Somaliland's population. The future of Somaliland rests on the shoulders of this group. Time and demography are in their favour. They also deserve far greater attention than is currently given.

Somaliland's youth came of age after the collapse of the military dictatorship. They were weaned on the hardship and sacrifice that followed Barre's campaigns against Northerners, life in refugee camps, and struggles during reconstruction. Most have close relatives who suffered for the second independence.

The youth have no memories of the old Somali Republic, only the ravages it left in its wake. A member of this group is Xasan Ibraahin Weedsame, a mathematics teacher in Hargeysa. He is also one of the most talented poets and songwriters in the Somali language today. Weedsame grew up after the ousting of the military dictator.

I saw a video of him speaking at a Somali function in London in 2014. He said something that captured the views of his generation: "I have no recall of the blue flag. I see myself as the flower that sprouted from the ashes of the old country."

Returning to the old order is untenable for Weedsame and those in his age group. They are preoccupied with issues affecting their lives – tribalism, poor education, unemployment, and migration.

Will a return to the old-world order with Mogadishu as the centre of the Somali universe help them? I believe not.

Third, honour women. There is a glaring gender gap in how credit is given for Somaliland's achievements. Since the end of Barre's rule, some heroes have fittingly earned tributes. Hargeysa alone has streets, schools, and other places named after veterans of the struggle. There are even books written about them. But the honour is one-sided. It went – and goes – only to men.

Yet women played a lion's role in the struggle. They also took part in the rebellion against Barre's despotic regime.

One mother of five illustrates the resilience and determination of women and the reason women should be extended much more credit. In the 1960s, this mother fled Kenya during the NFD crisis and built a new life in Somalia. She supported development initiatives, most notably the national literacy campaign to promote the Somali script. After completing the "national service," she attended college, married a schoolmate, and taught in public schools.

Barre's attacks on Hargeysa shattered her world. With her children in tow, she fled the bombing of Hargeysa and went to Ethiopia where she spent three years in a refugee camp in the Ogaden region. Soon after the SNM dislodged Barre's forces, she returned to the rubble, lived in a makeshift shelter for a year, and joined hands with other women and NGOs involved in school rehabilitation.

Somaliland gave her the most extended period of peace in a lifetime. She used the opportunity to invest in her children. She has a lawyer, a physician, an engineer, a public health specialist, and an environmentalist scientist.

I admire the achievement of this mother and praise the contributions of the women of this country.

Women juggled the many essential tasks thrust upon them. They are caregivers, counsellors, confidants, nurses, homemakers, breadwinners, livestock keepers, historians, fighters, and so on.

Khadra Cisman Cali, nicknamed the Libaaxo (Lioness), played a role in the struggle against Barre. Among other things, she supported the smuggling of SNM leaders to Ethiopia. There were many lionesses in Somaliland. Sahra Halgan joined the SNM movement while young. As a nurse, she tended to wounded fighters and saved many lives.

When Barre's security services rounded up members of the Ufo Association, women provided sustenance to the inmates in Hargeysa Prison. They also kept a vigil around the prison for days and nights and alerted the community when Barre's functionaries tried to smuggle the prisoners out of town late one night.

At the height of the Hargeysa bombing, women also saved many children. They strapped some on their backs, held others in tow, and braved the government shelling of the city. The flight from their homes took them to dusty refugee camps near the international border where new threats awaited. Malaria and vaccine-preventable diseases took a heavy toll on the children.

Women's work, of course, continued after the defeat of General Barre's forces. Women doubled as homemakers, caregivers, teachers, and builders in towns and cities ravaged by war. Without them, the story of the struggle would be incomplete. To these women, Somaliland owes a considerable debt.

Again, honour the women. Give them the credit they deserve.

Fourth, beware of environmental threats. Current trends in the degradation of the environment are alarming. Some rivers are dying, trees and wildlife are vanishing, and garbage accumulates in towns and villages.

No one escapes the blame for this situation – the nomads, urban dwellers, villagers, merchants, businesses, importers, politicians, and users of plastic products. The recent insults on the environment build on the legacy of colonialism, the war with Ethiopia, and the civil war. Unmitigated, the environmental problems may negate the hard-won gains of Somaliland and even threaten its survival.

Protect the environment. Reclaim the rivers, for they are the arteries of this arid land. Get a handle on plastic. Plant a tree every year. Push your political leaders to adopt the most ambitious water provision and conservation plans – something on the scale of Ethiopian's Grand Renaissance Dam Project! A society that spends USD 680 million annually on khat must re-examine its priorities.

And finally, advocate for the protection of public places and the creation of parks. Hargeysa's bustling neighbourhoods will become more unbearable and segregated without such places.

Epilogue

My notes provide updates on a few topics in the story. I prepared them in 2021, two years after my Somaliland visit. But surely, other significant changes will occur before this story is published.

Election fever gripped the Horn of Africa in 2021. Somalia missed its February date. The situation disappointed many, including Somalia's coaches on democracy.

Djibouti, Somaliland's neighbour to the northwest, held its presidential election in April 2021. Ismail Omar Geeleh declared victory, with ninety-seven per cent of the votes reportedly in his favour. He took the oath to serve his fifth consecutive term as president.

In May 2021, Somaliland went to the polls to elect parliamentarians and local government officials. Every national aged fifteen years or older could vote, and the state covered most of the expenses.

Britain and EU election observers commended Somaliland on the orderly election. Another visitor went further. "I have observed elections in many countries in Africa, but there was something unique about the process in Somaliland. There was not any violence or claims of rigging," said John Githongo, the former tzar on anti-corruption in President Mwai Kibaki's government in Kenya. "Based on this election," he continued, "I am wondering why Somaliland is yet to be recognised internationally with that level of democracy and organisation."

The opposition parties won the majority seats in Parliament and the hotly contested seat of speaker. Barkhad Batuun made history. This young attorney belongs to the Madhibaan community that has long endured discrimination. Batuun received most of his support from many young voters who wanted to make a statement against historical injustices.

Among the winners were youthful candidates. One of them was Cabdikariim Axmed Moogeh, the new mayor of Hargeysa. Hardly a month after taking office, he launched a massive clean-up of the Hargeysa River.

There was, however, a snag in the 2021 election. None of the eighty-two new members of Parliament was female. Only one of the 222 elected new local officials was female. Gender inequity remains more profound than anyone admitted before the election.

In commerce, Somaliland has reached another milestone. The new cargo terminal in Berbera can service large container ships. It has a seventeen-metre draft, a 400-metre quay, and three ship-to-shore (STS) gantry cranes. The port capacity has increased by more than threefold. It can manage 500,000 twenty-foot equivalent units (TEU) annually.

Although Somaliland managed the election well and has taken steps to grow its economy, the nation has vulnerabilities.

On 27 March 2021, my cell phone vibrated at dawn. The eldest son of my classmate, the dean of the Hargeysa Medical School, was on the line. Something was amiss. Suddenly, I was awake and fretful. I wanted it to be a pocket dial, so I dismissed it.

A few hours later, the phone glowed with new alerts. There were messages from relatives and friends in Hargeysa, Nairobi, and Dubai. I sat up and listened. The voices were trembling, the text dripping with prayers. Dr Diiriye died of complications of COVID-19. He was unvaccinated. Somaliland lost a national treasure. I lost a dear friend. My eyes swelled, and my fists clenched.

In a world with 126 million COVID-19 cases and 2.77 million deaths recorded as of late March 2021, the passing of one man in Somaliland is only a blip on the screen. Yet, there is more to this story than meets the eye. COVID-19 poses a double threat to a small nation with meagre resources. It has taken a toll on the leaders of the health sector. Social media buzzed in the last week of March with an update on the casualties. Four of the best minds in the medical profession were in hospital with COVID-19. Then came the announcement of Dr Diiriye's death. The entire nation was on edge.

The fear of COVID-19 was justified because Somaliland had many strikes against it. It could not freely deal with the international community, directly engage international financial institutions, and, in dealing with emergencies, address the World Health Forum in Geneva. Meanwhile, a stock of life-saving vaccines intended for Somaliland sat in a medical store in Mogadishu. A dose or two of the medicine could have saved lives. The COVID-19 epidemic has subsided, but the outbreaks and other threats will continue, and without international recognition, Somaliland remains one of the most vulnerable countries in the world.

Grieving the death of their mentor and being unable to remedy the isolation of Somaliland, Dr Diiriye's students did something that impressed me. Soon after the funeral, they set out to build a home for their dean. Several months after launching this initiative, the students had secured a plot, a contractor, and funding deducted from their meagre earnings. I followed their progress through my niece, Foosiya, a member of the 2018 class of the Hargeysa Medical School. I commend the young physicians for honouring their mentors. I also urge them to emulate his example.

In Ethiopia, war drums are beating again. A civil war broke out barely eighteen months after my transit stop at Addis Ababa. This conflict started before the country had recovered from two consecutive crises – an invasion of desert locusts that wiped out outcrops and the devastating effects of the COVID-19 epidemic.

There were reports of civilian massacres on both sides, the use of rape as a weapon of war, and a looming food crisis. The forecast for reconciliation of the warring parties, Tigray and the federal government, is gloomy. The country will reap staggering social and economic hardships as the war effort escalates. Furthermore, the conflict is unlikely to produce a meaningful victory. It will plant emotional injuries that may take a long time to heal.

I had modest goals when I set out on the two-week family trip to Somaliland, the land of my ancestors – meeting relatives and schoolmates, visiting childhood haunts, and introducing my daughter Mariam to a place of historical importance to our family. The trip went well. We had smooth sailing and not a day of inclement weather during our wanderings. We did it! I thought. But that was not so.

The trip stimulated a deep reflection about the place. Somaliland and I grew up together. I was six and Somaliland a few months old when I landed there to enter school. In the next fifty-plus years, I thrived. But Somaliland had a difficult childhood, a near-death experience, so the focus of my story shifted to cover the experiences of the country of my childhood.

Somaliland has risen from the ashes. It has had a thumping heart-beat for nearly thirty years although the world does not hear it. It is safe, energetic, self-reliant, and more democratic than many countries with a seat at the United Nations, thanks to local stewards (political, traditional, and religious leaders) and a resilient population. Somaliland also has a disciplined youth population. It now maintains a cordial relationship with Ethiopia, its former adversary.

Somaliland can do much more to harness its demographic potential and safeguard its fragile environment. But the country deserves international recognition.